AAO-7856

Save the Earth Science Experiments

Save the Earth Science Experiments

Science Fair Projects for Eco-Kids

Elizabeth Snoke Harris

LARK BOOKS
A Division of Sterling Publishing Co., Inc.
New York / London

Editors:
**Joe Rhatigan &
Rain Newcomb**

Creative Director:
Celia Naranjo

Art Director:
Robin Gregory

Illustrator:
Orrin Lundgren

Cover Designer:
Robin Gregory

Harris, Elizabeth Snoke, 1973-
  Save the Earth science experiments : science fair projects for eco-kids /
Elizabeth Snoke Harris ; illustrator, Orrin Lundgren. -- 1st ed.
      p. cm.
  Includes index.
  ISBN 978-1-60059-322-2 (hc-plc with jacket : alk. paper)
  1. Science projects--Juvenile literature. 2.
Science--Experiments--Juvenile literature. 3.
Environmentalism--Experiments--Juvenile literature. 4. Environmental
responsibility--Experiments--Juvenile literature. I. Lundgren, Orrin, ill.
II. Title.
  Q182.3.H377 2008
  507.8--dc22
                              2008017826

10 9 8 7 6 5 4 3 2 1

First Edition

Published by Lark Books, A Division of
Sterling Publishing Co., Inc.
387 Park Avenue South, New York, NY 10016

Text © 2008, Elizabeth Snoke Harris
Illustrations on pages 12, 15, 23, 27, 29, 31, 38, 39, 40, 42, 47, 55, 69, 72, 80, 89, 99 © Lark Books
Cover Photograph: © OJO Images

Distributed in Canada by Sterling Publishing,
c/o Canadian Manda Group, 165 Dufferin Street
Toronto, Ontario, Canada M6K 3H6

Distributed in the United Kingdom by GMC Distribution Services,
Castle Place, 166 High Street, Lewes, East Sussex, England BN7 1XU

Distributed in Australia by Capricorn Link (Australia) Pty Ltd.,
P.O. Box 704, Windsor, NSW 2756 Australia

If you have questions or comments about this book, please contact:
Lark Books
67 Broadway
Asheville, NC 28801
828-253-0467

Manufactured in China

ISBN 13: 978-1-60059-322-2

For information about custom editions, special sales, and premium and corporate purchases, please
contact Sterling Special Sales Department at 800-805-5489 or specialsales@sterlingpub.com

This book was printed on recycled paper using agri-based ink.

Contents

Save the Earth with Your Science Fair Project!

If you read the newspaper or watch the news, you can easily get overwhelmed by the laundry list of environmental problems we're facing these days: rising temperatures, severe storms, dangerous air, lack of clean drinking water, food shortages, fuel costs, and more.

How do we know about these problems? Through the curiosity of scientists and researchers around the world. Quite simply, they notice something peculiar (such as melting polar ice caps) and start asking questions about it. Then, they make observations, take measurements, seek answers, and announce their findings. Scientists know that knowledge is the key to finding solutions, and that it's often this search that keeps hope alive. *Save the Earth Science Experiments* is all about this process. It's a scientific journey into the different environmental crises we face and the ways you can actually make a difference.

Look around your home or school. Watch how you and others go through the day while you keep some of the world's problems in the back of your mind.

Start noticing the little things and form questions.

Just how much garbage does my family throw away, anyway?

How come we don't use the Sun's energy to heat our home?

Why do we keep using gas to fuel our car when I keep hearing about all these new alternative energies?

As soon as you tune in to what's going on around you and start getting curious, you're thinking like a scientist. And once you're thinking like a scientist you can do what scientists do: formulate answers to your questions, test your ideas through an experiment, evaluate what happened in your experiment, and then tell everyone what you found out.

These are the very steps you'll take to complete a science fair project. But since you care about the environment, this will be one science fair project that won't feel tedious and boring. You'll be making a difference.

This book is broken up into five chapters. The first chapter helps you with the details of doing a science fair project. The next four present more than 20 different experiments related to today's environmental issues that you can try—projects in which the questions are already formulated, but the answers are up to you. Each project gives you plenty of opportunities to work out some questions of your own (check out the "Explore Further" sections). Feel free to use the projects as is, but also be open to exploring other questions that come up as you read this book. We've also included several "Take Action" sections that list simple things you can do RIGHT NOW to start making a difference.

Throughout the book, you'll also find interesting articles on today's issues, along with photographs that take you around the world looking for solutions.

With the help of this book you will harness alternative energies from the wind, Sun, and water. You'll explore garbage and what happens once it lands in the trashcan. You'll examine the greenhouse effect and pollutants that cause global warming. You'll discover how much water you really need to use. But most important, you'll reach beyond today's depressing headlines—grabbing onto the hope that's there in simply looking for the answers. You'll be taking your first steps toward saving the Earth.

Good luck!

How to Make a Great Science Fair Project

Of course, the most important thing about your science fair project is that you're helping figure out how to save the Earth. But it wouldn't hurt to take home a blue ribbon too, would it? Here's what you need to do to have the best project at the science fair.

Ask a Question

Science experiments start with a question. And "how" is the word that scientists use most often—after all, science is the study of *how* things work. As you work on the question for your science fair experiment, use words such as "affect," "determine," "compare," and, of course, "how." Your question should not use words like "more," "better," or "which."

Really good science fair questions usually come in a specific form. For instance:

How does _____affect_____?

How does ____ determine _____?

Fill in the blanks with something you can measure, such as distance, time, weight, speed, temperature, or something else that can be counted.

Answer It

Once you have your question, you take an educated guess at the answer. This is called forming your *hypothesis*. It doesn't matter if your hypothesis is right or wrong—all you need to do is take your question and answer it.

A good hypothesis is the key to a successful science fair project, but remember, you don't need to invent a brand new fuel that will save the Earth. For your project to be a success, you need to ask a question that you can then answer by doing an experiment. (If you end up inventing a new fuel technology in the process, all the better.)

Suppose your question is "How does the shape of a solar cooker affect the temperature in the cooker?" Your hypothesis would either be:

*The shape of a solar cooker **does affect** the temperature in the cooker.*
or
*The shape of a solar cooker **does not affect** the temperature in the cooker.*

Research Your Topic

The Take a Closer Look section will give you some ideas for places to start your research. Get books from the library, talk to your science teacher about finding scientists you can interview, and look online for more

SUPER SCIENCE FAIR SECRET
Your hypothesis can be wrong and it won't count against you at the science fair. The judges want to see that you've asked a good question, designed a solid experiment, and worked carefully. Just write down the reasons you chose your hypothesis in your lab notebook!

resources. Write down everything you discover—and where you found it—in a lab notebook.

Design Your Experiment

The scientific method is a strategy scientists use to design experiments that will test their hypotheses. When you follow the scientific method, other scientists can duplicate your experiment. So, once you have your hypothesis, you're ready to design the experiment. There are three basic parts to every experiment. Identify them and write down each one in your lab notebook.

1. The Independent Variable

The *independent variable* is what you change in the experiment. This is usually the same thing as is in the first part of your question. In our example, that would be the shape of the solar cooker—rectangular or parabolic. Do you see how each project has only one independent variable?

2. The Dependent Variable

Decide what you're going to measure and how you're going to measure it. This is called the *dependent variable*. When you change your independent variable, your dependent variable will change, too. It depends on what happens to your independent variable. This is the same thing that is in the second part of your question. In our example, that would be the temperature inside the cooker.

3. The Controls

Finally, you need to decide what other variables you're going to control. That is, what other factors might affect the temperature inside your solar cooker? Make sure that these don't change during the experiment. These things are your *controls*. Everything that is not your dependent or independent variable is a control. Some variables to control might be the size of the cooker, the amount of sunlight, how long the cooker heats up, and the material it's made out of. That's a lot of stuff to keep track of. Don't forget to write it all down.

Do Your Experiment

You'll test each part of your experiment several times under the same conditions. Each time you repeat a part of your experiment is called a *trial*. The more trials you perform, the less chance there will be for error to creep into your experiment. Write down everything in your lab notebook. Make a data table before you start taking measurements and use a separate table for each trial. Leave lots of room in your table to record observations. You can even take pictures and draw diagrams.

Averages

During your experiment, you might take lots of measurements to cut down on error. If so, you'll need to calculate an average to combine all those measurements into a useable number. To do this, add up all the numbers up and divide by the total number of values you added. For example, if you measured the temperature change for the parabolic cooker to be 32, 28, 41 35, 32, and 36 degrees Fahrenheit, the average would be calculated like this:

$(32 + 28 + 41 + 35 + 32 + 36) \div 6 = 34$

This means that on average the temperature inside the parabolic cooker increased by an average of 34 degrees Fahrenheit.

Super Science Fair Secret
Do you have one or two really weird numbers that don't fit the pattern the rest of your data show? These are called *outliers*, and you can throw these away and retake that measurement.

Analyze Your Data

Once you've finished your experiment, you'll end up with a bunch of numbers—your data. You need to turn those numbers into something you can use to answer your question. First, look for patterns. Ask yourself: How did the dependent variable change with the independent variable? Next, you'll probably have to do a little math before you can analyze, or you might need to make a graph or table to see your data. (See page 102 for more information about that.)

Averaging lets you combine all the measurements from each trial into one number that you can use. In the example we've been using, you can *average* the temperatures for each type of solar cooker. That lets you compare two numbers (one for each type of cooker) instead of trying to compare two giant data tables. You can even display your data using a graph. This will make the next step much easier.

Write Your Report

After you've done all your hard work, it's time to show off what you learned. Most science fairs require a written report. This is simple—just look in your lab notebook. All that you'll need is probably already written down in there somewhere.

Title Page

This should be short and to the point. Your title shouldn't be longer than your report. You can even just use your research question for the title. Be sure to include your name, grade, the date, and your school on the title page.

Abstract

The purpose of the *abstract* is to give people an idea of what your project is about so they can decide whether they want to read the entire report. All you need are a few sentences that say what your project is about and what you found out.

Introduction

The introduction is where you explain what your project is all about. What question are you trying to answer? How did you choose this topic? Why is this an important subject to study? You can also include information you found in your research.

Procedure

Think of this section as a story about how you did your experiment rather than instructions for doing it again. Describe what you did, what you measured, and what materials you used. What were your dependent and independent variables? What were your controls and how did you control them? This is also a good place to put a drawing or photo of your setup. Be sure to label all the parts.

Data

This is where you put your graphs and data tables. However, if you made a graph of your data, you don't need a table with the same data. (See page 102 for more information about charts and graphs.) Make sure you have labels and don't forget the units of measurement.

Discuss Your Data

What do your graphs and tables show? Point out any patterns or trends you want the reader (or the judges) to notice. Describe your observations here too.

Conclusion

Here's your chance to explain what it all means and give the answer to your question. Is there anything you would do differently? Did you come up with more questions than answers? What are some ideas for further research?

References

Be sure to give proper credit. List all the books, web sites, and people you used for your research, as well as anyone who helped you do your experiment.

Wind Power
- Abstract
- Introduction
- Procedure
- Data
- Discuss Your Data
- Conclusion
- References

Put Together Your Display

For the actual science fair you'll need a display. This is usually a three-paneled, freestanding board that you can buy at most office and school supply stores. Be sure to check with your teacher for rules on space and size for your display so you don't get disqualified. Here are some tips for making a super display:

Less Is More

Don't cover your board with words. You need to leave something to talk about with the judges. Use lists instead of paragraphs. The judges don't have an hour to spend reading all the parts of your board.

Use Pictures

If you can use pictures instead of words to show your procedure and setup clearly, then do it. However, don't include extra pictures just for decoration. Every picture should be up there for a reason. Be sure to label the important parts of a picture or diagram that you want the judges to notice. Label where the picture came from too—did your Mom take it or did you download it from the Internet?

Keep It Simple

Make sure your board isn't crowded. Empty space is a good thing. Also pay attention to the colors you choose. Don't put pink words on a blue background or anything else that will make the judges cross-eyed.

Keep It Neat

Use a computer, word processor, or stencils to print out all the parts of your display so you don't have to worry about handwriting. Use rubber cement to attach paper to your board. (Glue can make the paper look crumpled.) Don't use staples; most boards aren't thick enough to hold them.

Before you glue everything down, have other folks (especially people who didn't help you perform the experiment) look at your display. Ask them if they can read everything, if it makes sense, and if anything is missing.

Check the Rules!

If you plan on including parts of your experiment with your display, check to make sure the rules allow this. Animals, even fish and insects, are usually restricted.

Your display board should include the following:

* **Title**
* **Problem/Question**
* **Hypothesis**
* **Abstract**
* **Description/Drawing/Photo of experimental setup**
* **Procedure**
* **Data, including graphs and tables (but graphs are usually better)**
* **Conclusions**
* **References**

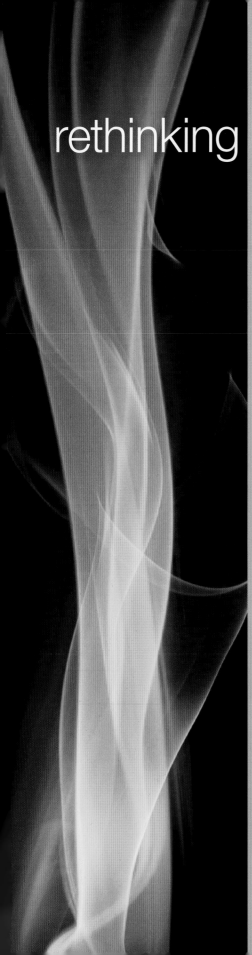

rethinking ENERGY

From eating dinner and listening to music to checking email and keeping the house warm, just about everything we do takes energy. And where we get our energy from is a huge environmental issue. For hundreds of years, we've relied on fossil fuels such as coal, oil, and natural gas to produce the energy we need. In the past few decades, we've started to realize that fossil fuels are creating major problems for the Earth.

Fossil fuels release energy AND carbon when they are burned. All that carbon contributes to the *greenhouse effect*—heating up the Earth and changing our global climate.

Unfortunately, global warming isn't the only problem due to the use of these fuels. Fossil fuels take thousands of years to make, and some day, we will run out. We need to find new sources of energy and reduce the amount of energy we use overall. When researchers evaluate alternative energies, there are a few important things they look for:

Will it provide enough energy?

If an alternative energy is going to replace fossil fuels, it has to provide enough energy to do the work the fossil fuels were doing.

Is it a renewable resource?

An alternative energy should be something we can get power from for years to come. Switching to a new source of energy that will run out in a few years isn't a good long-term solution to our energy needs.

How much does it pollute?

Does the alternative energy pollute when it creates power? If the new energy pollutes just as much as the old one, it's not a very good solution.

How easy is it to gather?

In the process of drilling for more oil and mining for more coal we're tearing up the environment, destroying forests, mountains, and other ecosystems. Alternative energies need to avoid this problem.

How easy is it to use?

If a new fuel takes a lot of money or resources to be converted into energy we can use, it's not going to work. Alternative energies need to be inexpensive to produce and easy to use.

Several different sources of energy, such as solar and wind power, biofuels, and hydrogen power, are explored in this chapter. There are also projects that investigate how we can conserve (use less) energy.

Alternative Oils

etroleum oil is one of our primary fossil fuels. We use it to run our cars, heat our homes, and, in some places, to create electricity. When petroleum is burned, it produces energy *and* puts a lot of carbon dioxide into the atmosphere. (Petroleum also takes thousands years to make, so when we run out of oil, it'll be a long time before the Earth makes more.) But you have to go to school, stay warm in the winter, and have enough light to do your homework. So what can you do?

One solution is to use a different kind of oil that pollutes less and comes from a renewable source. Many people believe oils from plants such as corn, rapeseed, sugar cane, and others offer a cleaner alternative. But do these plant oils (known as *biofuel*) produce about the same amount of usable energy as petroleum oil?

JUST THE FACTS

* Burning 1 gallon (3.8 l) of gas puts 20 pounds (9 kg) of carbon dioxide in the air.

* In 2006, the United States burned 388 million gallons (1,468 million l) of gas every day, putting nearly 8 billion pounds (3.5 billion kg) of carbon dioxide in the atmosphere daily.

* The amount of gasoline the United States uses is more than four times the combined total of what China and Japan use daily—and those countries have five times as many people as the United States.

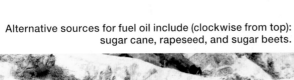

Alternative sources for fuel oil include (clockwise from top): sugar cane, rapeseed, and sugar beets.

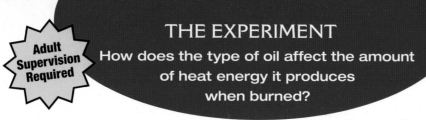

THE EXPERIMENT
How does the type of oil affect the amount of heat energy it produces when burned?

Adult Supervision Required

Summary

You'll burn vegetable and petroleum oils and compare how well they heat water.

What You Need

- Bucket of sand
- Paper clip
- Heavy cotton rope
- Scissors
- Eyedropper
- Vegetable oil
- Ring stand*
- Metal soup can
- Measuring cup
- Water
- Styrofoam cup**
- Glass thermometer
- Matches
- Stopwatch
- #20 or #30 automobile oil

* You can get a ring stand from your science teacher or from a science supply store.

** Reuse an old foam cup or use a new one made from biodegradable foam.

Experimental Procedure

Note: Keep the bucket of sand nearby to extinguish the burning oil if necessary. Do not pour water on burning oil. Do this experiment on a countertop that you've completely cleared off.

1. Bend the middle piece of the paper clip straight up. Separate the rest of the clip so that it makes a stand with the middle piece pointing straight up.

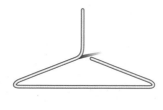

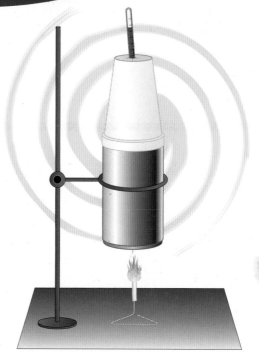

2. Use the scissors to cut a 1-inch (3 cm) piece of heavy cotton rope. Slide it over the upright part of your paper clip stand.

3. Use the dropper to put 20 drops of vegetable oil on the rope. Make sure all the oil soaks into it.

4. Place the oil-soaked rope and paper clip stand under the ring stand. Place the can in the ring stand and fill it with ¼ l of water.

5. Place the foam cup upside down over the can. Poke the thermometer through the top of the cup. The bottom of the thermometer should be in the can, but not touching it. You should see enough of the thermometer sticking out of the cup to read the temperature of the water.

6. Read the initial temperature of the water in degrees Celsius. Write it down in your lab notebook.

7. Light the oil-soaked rope and let it burn completely. Let it go out by itself. Use the stopwatch to time how long it takes to burn.

8. When the rope has finished burning, read and write down the final temperature of the water in degrees Celsius. Subtract the initial temperature from the final temperature to find the change in temperature caused by the burning vegetable oil.

9. Repeat steps 2 through 8 at least four more times using the vegetable oil. Then repeat the process five times using the petroleum oil.

Conclusion

Average the temperature change (from step 8) for each type of oil. How do the temperatures compare? The amount the temperature of the water changes is related to how much energy the different oils produced when burned. The greater the change in temperature, the greater the output of energy. You can use the average change in temperature to calculate the amount of energy each oil produced.

Energy is measured in calories, whether it's the energy created by burning oil or the energy you get from eating food. This is the formula:

Energy = (mass) x (change in temperature) x (specific heat)

So to calculate the number of calories produced by oil, you'll need the following:

- the mass of the water (.25 liter of water has a mass of 250 grams),
- the change in temperature of the water (you already have that),
- the specific heat of water (0.001 calories/(g°C). (This is how much energy it takes to raise the temperature of 1 gram of water by 1°C.)

So if the average temperature change of the water heated by burning vegetable oil is 4°C, then the energy produced is:

(250 g) x (4°C) x 0.001 calories/(g°C) = 1 calorie

Once you've calculated the energy released in calories for each type of oil, make a bar graph of oil type versus energy. How do the energies compare?

Average the burn time for each type of oil. How do the times compare? Which oil released the most energy when burned? Which oil released its energy the quickest? Would vegetable oil be a good substitute for petroleum oil as a fuel?

This is an ethanol plant, where corn is converted to fuel.

Take a Closer Look

Oil is a *hydrocarbon*, or a complex molecule made of carbon and hydrogen atoms. When it burns, the hydrocarbon combines with oxygen to make carbon dioxide and water. This chemical reaction releases a whole lot of heat energy. The amount of energy and carbon dioxide released by a burning hydrocarbon is determined by the arrangement and the number of carbon and hydrogen atoms in the oil molecule.

From animal parts left over from a processing plant to raw sewage, just about any organic material can be made into oil. Organic materials are anything made out of carbon and hydrogen.

Vegetable oil is made by pressing vegetables—literally squeezing the oil out of them. Petroleum oil forms deep inside the Earth. Heat and pressure squeeze dinosaur remains (and ancient organic matter in the soil) until they turn into oil. Humans use another process, called *thermal conversion*, to copy this method. The difference is that thermal conversion takes a few hours in a factory to produce oil instead of a thousands of years deep underground. In both cases, heat and pressure push on the organic material until the carbon, hydrogen, and oxygen break apart and join back together to form oil hydrocarbons. The oil made by thermal conversion can be converted to electricity. All of the leftover parts, like the calcium in animal bones, are used to make fertilizer.

Some people make their own biofuel at home, using leftover vegetable oil from restaurants. You can modify the engine of your car to do this, or you can process the used vegetable oil, turning it into a biofuel. So the next time you go out to eat, go ahead and order the French fries— you may be helping to fuel someone's car.

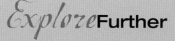

Many countries, especially in Europe, are growing rapeseed for fuel. It's relatively cheap to grow and it yields a respectable amount of oil.

*Explore***Further**

Try other types of oil such as peanut, olive, or corn oil. Is there a difference in the amount of heat produced by solid animal fats, such as lard, and the liquid oils?

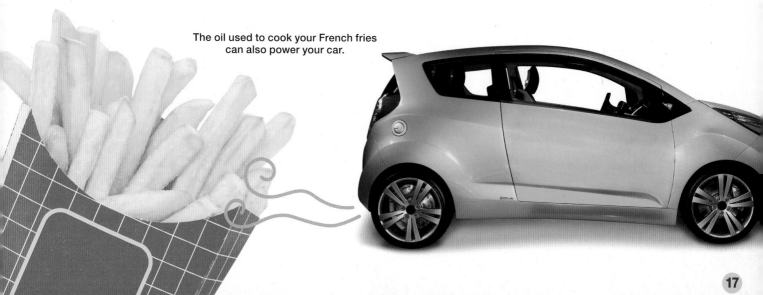

The oil used to cook your French fries can also power your car.

The High Price of Ethanol

Ethanol is one of the most popular biofuels. It's made mostly from corn but it can also be produced from other materials such as palm trees, sugar cane, wood chips, or grass. It's used to replace petroleum gasoline made from fossil fuels, but is it really a better fuel?

The biggest advantage of ethanol is that it's a renewable energy. You can always grow more corn to make more ethanol. Once you've pumped all the oil out of the Earth, it's gone (at least for a few thousand years until the Earth makes more). When ethanol was first developed, people were really excited about it because it seemed that, overall, ethanol releases fewer greenhouse gases than gasoline because the corn uses up carbon dioxide as it grows.

However, ethanol isn't necessarily the solution to our fuel problems. Scientists have now found that ethanol actually creates *more* greenhouse gases than gasoline if you look at the whole process of creating and using it as a fuel.

Here are some of the issues that need to be addressed:

- Cars that run on ethanol get fewer miles per gallon so it takes more fuel to get where you're going.
- It takes a lot of fertilizer to grow corn. Much of this fertilizer gets washed into rivers, lakes, and even the ocean. Fertilizer in the water causes problems for the plants and animals that live there. (See the Deadly Fertilizer project on page 98 for more about this.)
- Diverting land and plants usually reserved for the global food supply to fuel cars is raising food prices and creating shortages in various regions of the world.
- Farmers in Asia, South America, and other parts of the world are cutting down forests and plowing up grasslands to make room to grow more palm trees and corn. Destroying the forests and grasslands releases greenhouse gases as they are burned and plowed under. To make things worse, the corn and palm trees that are planted on the cleared land soak up only a small part of the greenhouse gases compared to the dense rain forests and grasslands that used to grow there.

The most promising possibility is to find a way to make ethanol out of agricultural waste—all the parts of crop plants not used for food.

Power Plants

As noted in the previous project, biofuels are created from plants. When plants and plant oils are burned, they release energy we can use. The amount of a plant's potential biofuel is called its *biomass*. Scientists are experimenting with different plants to see which will provide the most biomass with the least amount of effort (time, resources, etc.).

JUST THE FACTS

* To grow, plants convert sunlight, water, and carbon dioxide into energy.

* Using biofuels still releases carbon into the atmosphere, but plants also suck carbon out of the atmosphere while they're growing.

* Soils and plant material store 2.7 times more carbon than is in the air.

* Biofuels provide about 86% of all the energy used in Burundi, Sudan, Botswana, and Sierra Leone.

* Pakistan, Myanmar, and Thailand rely on just one biofuel source—wood—to produce more than half of the energy those nations consume annually.

* A combination of biofuels provides about 3% of the energy used in the United States.

THE EXPERIMENT
How does the type of plant affect the amount of biomass it produces?

Summary

You'll grow several types of grass and measure how much biomass each one produces.

What You Need

- 3 medium pots with drainage holes
- Potting soil
- Wheat or rye seed
- Corn seed
- Whole oats
- Water
- Fluorescent grow lamp
- Paper towels
- Scale
- Cookie sheets
- Oven (optional)

Experimental Procedure

1. Fill the pots with potting soil.

2. Count out 30 seeds of each type of grass you're using. Plant the seeds about 1 inch (2.5 cm) under the soil.

3. Water the pots. Throughout the experiment, water the pots as needed. The soil should be moist but not wet.

4. Place the pots under the grow lamp. Use the ruler to make sure each pot is 4 inches (10.2 cm) from the lamp. As the plants grow, keep moving the lamp so that remains 4 inches (10.2 cm) from the top of the plants.

5. Make a table to keep track of how your plants are growing. Record the date you planted the seeds and observe them every day until each has sprouted. Write down the day of the 1st, 10th, and 20th sprout for each type of grass.

6. After the grasses sprout, measure the height of the plants every two days. Measure and write down the average height of each type of grass.

7. After two weeks, pull all of the plants out of the pots. Get as much of the root as you can. Keep each type of plant separate.

8. Wash off the dirt and pat the plants dry with a paper towel.

9. Weigh all the plants of each type and write down the weights in your lab book.

10. Lay the plants on cookie sheets. Put the cookie sheets out in the sunshine and let the plants dry until they are crispy. If it's not sunny enough to dry the grasses, use an oven to dry them. Set the oven at 150°F (65°C), and keep an eye on them so they don't burn!

11. Carefully weigh the dry plants. Write the weights in your lab book. This is the final biomass for each type of plant.

The Carbon Cycle

Carbon doesn't stay in one place. It moves through the air, water, soil, plants, and animals, bonding with many different molecules. The carbon cycle is the path that carbon takes as it circulates throughout the planet and the atmosphere.

Carbon is released into the atmosphere when animals breathe and when plants and animals decay. Volcanoes also release carbon. The carbon gets sucked out of the atmosphere when plants use it to photosynthesize sunlight or the ocean and rocks absorb it.

Ideally, carbon moves into each of these areas at the same rate it moves out. However, extra carbon is released into the atmosphere every time fossil fuels are burned. As we use more and more fossil fuels, more and more carbon (in the form of the greenhouse gas carbon dioxide) is getting trapped in the atmosphere. There aren't enough plants, oceans, and rocks to absorb all this extra carbon.

One way to counteract this buildup of carbon is to create a *carbon sink*. A carbon sink uses the carbon cycle to get rid of excess carbon in the atmosphere. Trees are the most efficient carbon sinks. People, organizations, and towns calculate how much carbon they put into the atmosphere. Then they figure out how many trees they need to plant to soak it up. Cities in the United Kingdom, Australia, and Canada have begun planting trees to create carbon sinks.

*Explore*Further

Let the plants in your experiment grow for four weeks or even longer. How are the results different when the plants have more time to grow? What other factors affect the amount of biomass produced? Experiment with the type and amount of light, temperature, soil type, fertilizer, plant hormone, and seed depth. You can even study how the amount of carbon dioxide in the air affects plant growth by sealing the plants in a clear plastic bag with a bowl of baking soda and vinegar.

Try other grasses such as barley or rice. Or try burning the dried grasses to see which produces the most heat energy (see the Burning Oils project on page 14 for ideas on measuring the amount of heat).

Conclusion

Make a bar graph of plant type versus the date to the 1st, 10th, and 20th sprout. Which plants sprouted the quickest and which sprouted the slowest?

Make a line graph of day versus plant height for each type of plant. Which plant grew the tallest?

Make a bar graph of seed type versus final wet weight. Make another bar graph of seed type versus final dry weight. How do these graphs compare? Which plant produced the most biomass from sunlight energy? How does this compare to the rate at which the seeds sprouted and the height of the plants?

Take a Closer Look

Biomass can be used to make fuel and products that would otherwise be made from fossil fuels.

When biofuels are burned, they produce just as much carbon dioxide as fossil fuels. The difference is that when plants grow, they turn the carbon dioxide and energy from the Sun into their food. So, when the plants used to produce the biofuel are growing, they absorb carbon dioxide. This means that overall, biofuels put less carbon dioxide into the atmosphere than fossil fuels, right? Not necessarily. When you take into account the carbon dioxide released when the plants are grown (think tractors, fertilizer), you'll find that biofuels may release more carbon dioxide than petroleum.

A Bright Idea

Have you ever singed your fingers trying to replace a light bulb that's just burnt out? If a light bulb is supposed to be lighting up, why is it heating up, too? Is all that extra heat just a waste of precious energy?

JUST THE FACTS

* 10% of the electricity used in your house powers the lights.

* Incandescent light bulbs waste 90% of their energy as heat.

* Compact fluorescent (CFL) light bulbs use 60% less energy than a regular incandescent light bulb and last 10 times longer.

* By replacing just one incandescent bulb with a CFL bulb, your family will keep 300 pounds (136 kg) of carbon dioxide out of the air each year.

* Replacing all the light bulbs in the United States with CFL bulbs would reduce carbon-dioxide pollution by more than 90 billion pounds (40 billion kg).

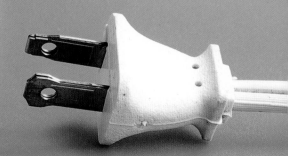

THE EXPERIMENT
How does the type of light bulb affect the amount of electricity it uses?

Summary

You'll use an electric meter to measure the amount of current used by an incandescent, halogen, and compact fluorescent light bulb.

What You Need

- Old working lamp that you can dismantle*
- Wire cutter
- Multimeter (or an ammeter and voltmeter)**
- 6-volt battery
- 60-watt incandescent light bulb
- Wires with alligator clips***
- 60-watt halogen light bulb
- 13-watt compact fluorescent light bulb

* You won't be able to put this lamp back together again. If you don't have one, you can get a lamp kit from the hardware store.

** You can get one of these at an electronics supply store.

*** These may already be attached to your meter.

Experimental Procedure

1. Plug in the old lamp to make sure it works before going to the next step. If you're using a lamp kit, follow the directions to assemble the lamp. (You can skip the steps involved with attaching the kit to a lamp base.) Then plug it into the wall to make sure it really works.

2. Unplug the lamp. Use the wire cutters to cut the cord about 6 inches (15.2 cm) from the plug. Split the wire (it's actually two wires stuck together) and separate them for 6 to 8 inches (15.2 to 20.3 cm).

3. Use the wire cutter to carefully strip about 1 inch (2.5 cm) of the plastic casing from both wire ends.

4. Use your multimeter to measure the voltage of the battery before you continue with the experiment. Put one lead from the meter on the positive terminal of the battery and the other on the negative terminal. It should read 6 volts.

If not, change the settings on the multimeter. Write down the voltage in your lab book and unhook the wires.

5. Place the incandescent light bulb in your lamp and screw it in tightly. Make sure the lamp is turned off before proceeding.

6. Wrap one of the exposed wires from the lamp around the negative terminal of the battery. Clip one of the leads from your multimeter to the other exposed wire. Clip the other meter lead to the positive terminal of the battery. Now you have what's called a "closed loop."

7. Make sure your meter is set to read the lowest value of current and turn on the lamp.

8. Adjust the settings on your meter until you can read the current going through the lamp. Your light bulb won't get enough energy from the 6-volt battery to light up, but current is still running through the bulb. Write down the current that the light bulb draws in your lab notebook.

9. Repeat steps 4 through 8 for the halogen and compact fluorescent light bulbs.

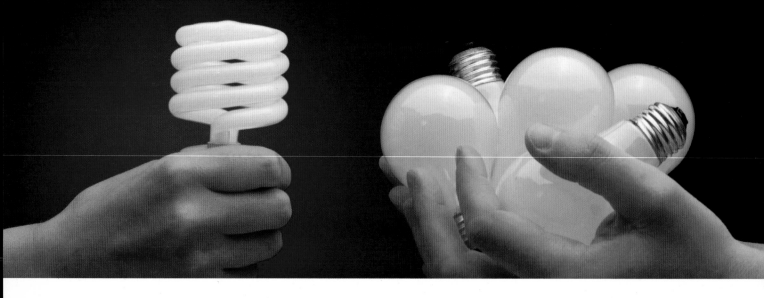

Conclusion

Make a bar graph of light bulb type versus current. Because you used the same voltage battery for each light bulb, the current is directly proportional to the power used by each light bulb. Which bulb used the most current and which used the least?

Take a Closer Look

What makes a light bulb glow—current or voltage? It turns out that you need both.

Voltage is a measure of how much energy is being used by the light bulb. In your experiment, electrons flowed from the battery through the light bulb. The light bulb used the energy in the electrons to light up. The flow of electrons is called *electric current*.

The battery you used only produced 6 volts of energy, which wasn't enough to fully power the light bulbs. (That's why they barely glowed.) The outlets in the wall deliver 120 volts in North and South America (and up to 240 volts in other countries), which is more than enough energy to make the bulbs glow brightly. When you connected the battery to the light bulb in a closed circuit (a big loop that connects the negative terminal of the battery to the light bulb back to the positive terminal), electrons flowed through the circuit. This flow of electrons, or current, is measured in *amperes* (*amps*). Different types of light bulbs use the energy in different ways to make light.

Look at the packaging for your light bulbs to find the power rating. (Note: This power rating is for when the light bulb is plugged into an outlet that supplies a lot more voltage than the 6-volt battery did.) The incandescent and halogen bulbs have a much higher wattage than the CFL bulb, but they all have the same brightness. This is because the CFL uses much less current to light the bulb, even though all the bulbs use the same voltage.

A better measure of brightness is *luminosity*, which is measured in *lumens*. In general, about 850 lumens is the brightness of a 60-watt incandescent light bulb. What were the luminosity ratings of the light bulbs you used?

*Explore***Further**

Investigate the current used by other bulb types such as those using light emitting diodes (LEDs) or the new incandescent light bulbs that claim to use less power.

Investigate the color of the light given off by the bulb. Some appear more bluish while others are more yellow. Look on the bulb packaging for the color rating. If you have access to a light meter (borrow one from a photographer) you can also compare the brightness of each bulb.

How much heat do the different types of light bulbs produce? How is this related to the current drawn? You can use each light bulb to heat a can of water just like in the experiment on page 15.

How Do Light Bulbs Work?

Incandescent

Look closely inside a clear incandescent light bulb. Can you see the glass rod in the center with two wires coming out of the base? Between the wires runs a tightly wound V-shaped coil. This coil is the *filament*, made of tungsten (a metal with one of the highest melting points). The current (or electrons) runs from one wire through the filament and down the other wire. The filament is so thin that the current can't go through easily and the metal heats up. As the metal gets hotter, it begins to glow brighter and brighter. Most of the energy actually goes into heat instead of light, and these bulbs will only last for about 1,000 hours. As the bulb burns, the tungsten from the filament evaporates. You can see this as a gray film on the inside of the bulb. Eventually the filament gets so thin it breaks and the light bulb burns out.

Halogen

A halogen lamp also uses a tungsten filament, but the filament is covered by a much smaller quartz envelope filled with gas—sort of like a mini-light bulb inside the bigger bulb. As the filament burns, it evaporates, forming a gray film on the inside of the envelope. The gas inside is a type of *halogen* (such as fluorine or chlorine). Halogen gases have a very interesting property:

When the temperature gets high enough, the halogen gas combines with evaporating tungsten and puts it back on the filament. This recycling process extends the life of the filament and lets it get much hotter, which means it produces more light using less energy. Halogen light bulbs still produce heat though, and because the quartz envelope is so close to the filament, it gets much hotter than an incandescent light bulb.

(Compact Fluorescent) CFL

Fluorescent bulbs use a completely different method to produce light. There are electrodes at both ends of a fluorescent tube. The tube is filled with argon and mercury gases. A current of electrons flows from one electrode to the other, passing through the gas. The electrons give energy to the gases in the tube and the gases release the energy as ultraviolet light. This ultraviolet light reacts with the phosphor coating inside of the fluorescent tube, and this phosphor creates visible light.

Most of the energy in a fluorescent bulb is used to make light and not heat, so it's up to six times more efficient than incandescent bulbs. It uses much less current to make the same amount of light. That's why a 15-watt fluorescent bulb produces the same amount of light as a 60-watt incandescent bulb. They can also last up to 10 times longer than an incandescent bulb.

take action

Switch to CFL bulbs in your home. You'll be helping to keep greenhouse gases out of the atmosphere (and save money on your electric bill). CFL bulbs can be expensive, so replace bulbs as they burn out. Make sure you take burned-out CFL bulbs to a collection site: they're considered hazardous due to their mercury content.

Organize a light bulb exchange. Talk to your local power company or go online to locate sponsors who will donate CFL bulbs. Set up a booth at your school or a local store and give a CFL bulb to everyone who brings in an energy-sucking incandescent bulb.

Running on Air

What if cars could run on air? It sounds crazy, but fuel-cell technology is attempting to make that a reality with cars that run on hydrogen gas—and the only waste is water. Of course, if this technology was cheap, simple, and/or readily available, every car exhaust pipe on the highway would be emitting water instead of toxic fumes. Researchers think they're getting closer to making hydrogen power a reality, but it may be another 15 years before you can brag about drinking your car's exhaust.

JUST THE FACTS

* Gasoline-powered cars emit harmful substances such as hydrocarbons, nitrogen oxide (which contributes to acid rain), and carbon monoxide.

* About half of the United States population breaths air that's so polluted it's been proven to harm human health and damage the environment. Chinese and Indian cities average four to seven times as much hazardous air pollution—affecting nearly 1 billion people.

* A gasoline engine turns less than 20% of its fuel into power.

* A hydrogen fuel cell turns 50% of its fuel into power.

This bicycle, created and produced by a company called Shanghai Pearl Hydrogen, relies on pedal power and hydrogen power.

THE EXPERIMENT
How does the amount of salt in a water solution affect how much hydrogen gas is produced through electrolysis?

Adult Supervision Required

Summary

You'll use electricity to break water into hydrogen and oxygen gases. Then you'll change the amount of salt in the water to see what effect this has on how much gas is produced.

What You Need

- Salt
- Measuring spoons
- Measuring cup
- Water
- 2 glasses
- Permanent marker and masking tape
- Wire cutters
- Two 8-inch (15.2 cm) lengths of plastic-coated copper wire
- Graphite rods (or 2 lead pencils sharpened on both ends)
- Electrical tape
- 9-volt battery
- Beaker or clear glass
- Test tube
- Stopwatch

*Safety Alert - This experiment must be performed in a well-ventilated room with open windows.

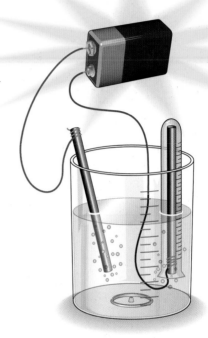

Experimental Procedure

1. To make a 5% salt solution, mix ¾ tablespoon (11.1 ml) of salt and 1 cup (236.6 ml) of water together in the first glass. Mix 1½ tablespoons (22.2 ml) of salt with 1 cup (236.6 ml) of warm water in the other glass to make a 10% salt solution. Label the glasses with the marker and masking tape so you don't get them mixed up.

2. Use the wire cutters to remove about 1 inch (2.5 cm) of the plastic coating from the ends of both pieces of copper wire.

3. Wrap the end of one wire around the end of one graphite rod (or pencil). Use a small piece of electrical tape to hold the wire in place. Do the same thing with the other rod and the other wire. If you're using a pencil, make sure the metal from the wire is touching the pencil lead (graphite).

4. Take the loose ends of the wires and wrap them around the leads on the battery. Put one on the positive end and one on the negative. You can use electrical tape to hold the wires in place if needed.

5. Fill the beaker about half full with plain water. Place the rods in the beaker. After several seconds, you'll see bubbles covering the rods. The bubbles on the rod connected to the negative lead of the battery are hydrogen. The bubbles on the rod connected to the positive lead of the battery are oxygen.

6. Remove the rods and fill the test tube with water.

7. Carefully lower the test tube into the beaker of water so that it's completely covered, and then turn it upside down so that it stays full of water. (A few tiny bubbles are fine.) It's okay if the end of the test tube is above the top of the water as long as no air is let into the test tube.

8. Slide the rod connected to the negative lead into the underwater test tube so that the wire end of the rod is pointing down and the other tip of the rod is pointing up into the test tube. Put the other rod in the water and start your stopwatch. The hydrogen gas bubbles will be trapped in the test tube.

9. After 15 minutes have passed, use the transparency marker to mark the water level on the test tube.

10. Remove the rods and test tube and pour the water down the drain. Rinse off and dry the graphite rods.

11. Measure how far from the bottom of the tube the gas reached. (If your test tube has volume markings printed on its side, use the markings to take your measurements.) Write the measurement down in your lab book.

12. Repeat steps 5 through 11, testing the 5% and then the 10% salt solution. Before you start, stir each solution well to dissolve any salt that may have settled out. Remember to fill the test tube with the same solution that's in the beaker.

Conclusion

Make a line graph of percent salt solution (the plain water is 0% salt) versus the amount of gas produced in 15 minutes. Which solution produced the most gas? Which produced the least? How much gas do you think would be produced by a 20% salt solution? Is this an efficient way of producing hydrogen gas?

Take a Closer Look

Water is a combination of two hydrogen (H) atoms and one oxygen (O) atom. (The short way to write this is H_2O.) When you zap the water with electricity, the hydrogen and oxygen atoms in the water break apart. The bubbles on the rod connected to the negative lead were hydrogen. The bubbles on the rod connected to the positive lead were oxygen.

You probably noticed that there were many more hydrogen bubbles than oxygen bubbles. Water has twice as many hydrogen atoms as oxygen, so it will release twice as much hydrogen gas.

So what does salt have to do with all this? The salt is an *electrolyte*, which helps the water conduct electricity more easily. This means that more electrical energy passes through the water, which makes the water molecules break up more quickly.

Once you add salt to the solution, the oxygen bubbles aren't just oxygen. They contain chlorine from the salt. In this experiment, you won't be producing very much chlorine gas, but it is poisonous. That's why you did this experiment with plenty of ventilation.

Explore Further

Try other electrolytes besides salt, such as baking soda (aka sodium bicarbonate), sulfuric acids, and other salts such as potassium chloride (light salt) or calcium chloride (road salt).

What happens if you use different materials for the leads instead of graphite? Try paper clips, copper wire, or iron nails.

Test the gases to make sure they are really hydrogen and oxygen. To do this, light a long match, let it burn for a few seconds, and then blow it out. Immediately place it in the mouth of the test tube of gas. If it's oxygen, the match will start to glow brightly. If it's hydrogen, you'll hear a loud pop. The pop is the hydrogen reacting with oxygen to form water again. This process releases energy and is the basis for hydrogen fuel cells.

How Hydrogen Powered Cars Work

Hydrogen-powered cars use a fuel cell, called an *electrochemical energy conversion device*. The fuel cell turns the hydrogen and oxygen into water. The energy released in this chemical reaction is electricity. So, basically, the fuel cell reverses what you did in the experiment on page 27. Instead of using electricity to break water into hydrogen and oxygen, it combines hydrogen and oxygen, making water and releasing electricity.

The most common fuel cell for use in cars and other applications is called the *Polymer Exchange Membrane (PEM)* fuel cell. To get enough electricity to run a car, several of these single cells are combined in a *fuel cell stack*. Keep an eye out for fuel-cell cars on a road near you. They may be coming soon.

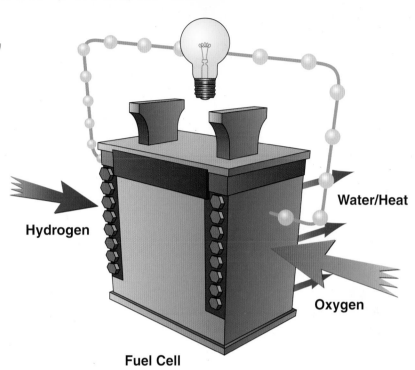

Hydrogen

Water/Heat

Oxygen

Fuel Cell

How Green is Hydrogen Power?

Hydrogen is an energy carrier, not an energy source. The energy to make a hydrogen fuel cell go ultimately has to come from a power plant, because you have to make the hydrogen before you can use it in your hydrogen car. Hydrogen can be produced from water by electrolysis, but the electricity still has to come from somewhere. If the electricity comes from renewable energy such as solar, water, or wind power instead of burning fossil fuels, the process of creating a hydrogen fuel cell would release no carbon dioxide.

The Sun Solution

There's a giant power source 93 million miles (150 million km) away from us—the Sun! Plants turn sunlight directly into energy they can use, and we can do the same. Solar panels, also called *photovoltaic cells*, convert light into electricity. Solar power is free and, for the next eight million years, renewable. Solar cells are used for traffic signs on the highway, in calculators, on houses, and for many other things, including the International Space Station. (Which is a good thing, since there isn't an extension cord long enough to reach the space station.)

JUST THE FACTS

* Sunlight takes about eight minutes to travel 93 million miles (150 million km) from the Sun to the Earth.

* In one hour, the Earth receives more energy from the Sun than the entire population of the world could use in a year.

* The first photovoltaic module (solar panel) was built in 1954.

* Photovoltaic cells currently provide 0.04% of the world's energy.

* In 1990, an aircraft flew 2,500 miles (4,000 km) across the United States, using only solar power.

* To completely power your house, you'd need a solar panel about 24 feet long by 10 feet high (7.3 m by 3 m). It would provide 2,000 watts of electricity.

* Each month this solar panel would:

  – replace the power generated by 150 pounds (70 kg) of coal

  – prevent 300 pounds (130 kg) of carbon dioxide from entering the atmosphere when that coal was burned to create electricity

  – save the 105 gallons (400 l) of water that would be used to mine and process the coal.

Solar panels take advantage of Earth's most cost-effective power source—the Sun!

THE EXPERIMENT
How does the brightness of a light source affect the amount of energy a photovoltaic cell produces?

Summary

You'll shine light bulbs of different brightness ratings on a photovoltaic cell and use a multimeter to measure how much current is produced.

What You Need

- Multimeter (or ammeter)* Alligator clip test lead*
- Photovoltaic cell (solar panel) rated at 3 volts and 100 mA*
- LED (light emitting diode)*
- 5 light bulbs with different light ratings (given in lumens on the package)
- Gooseneck lamp
- Ruler

* You can get all of these items at an electronics supply store.

Experimental Procedure

1. Set the multimeter to measure DC current in the 200 mA range. This setting allows the multimeter to read the small amount of direct current generated by your cell.

2. Use one alligator clip test lead to connect the red wire of the photovoltaic cell to the long lead of the LED. Connect the red probe of the multimeter to the short lead of the LED. Then attach the black probe of the multimeter to the black wire of the photovoltaic cell. You've just made a series circuit.

3. Put the brightest light bulb in the gooseneck lamp. Use the ruler to position it exactly 12 inches (30.5 cm) above the photovoltaic cell. Turn it on.

4. The LED should light up. If it doesn't, recheck all of your connections you created in step 2. Make sure your multimeter is working.

5. Write down the current reading (in amps) on the multimeter and the lumens rating of the light bulb. You can find the brightness in lumens printed on the light bulb package. If the value of the current is too low to read, switch the multimeter to the next lowest setting. This will make the multimeter more sensitive to the amount of current the photovoltaic cell is producing.

6. Turn off the lamp and wait for the bulb to cool down. Unplug the lamp and take out the bulb. Then put in the next brightest bulb and repeat steps 3 to 5.

7. Repeat step 6 to test the amount of current each light bulb produces.

Conclusion

Make a graph of current in amps versus light bulb brightness in lumens.

The light bulbs with a higher brightness rating will shine more light on the photovoltaic cell. How is the amount of light that hits the photovoltaic cell related to the amount of current produced?

Take a Closer Look

Photovoltaic cells are made from semiconductors. When the light hits the cell, the semiconductor absorbs the light energy and some of the semiconductor's electrons are knocked loose. Electric fields in the photovoltaic cells direct the electrons to wires on the top and bottom of the cell so that they can flow out as electric current. The electric current can be used to light up LEDs or whatever else the photovoltaic cell is hooked up to.

New Technologies

You don't have to put solar panels all over your house to take advantage of free energy from the Sun. Every day, more and more technologies are being developed that use solar power. Here are just a few:

- Solar lights for your walkway. The photovoltaic cells produce energy during the day and light up at night.
- Solar-powered battery rechargers. Charge up your batteries with the Sun.
- Solar-powered lamps. Save up light from the Sun during the day and use it at night.
- Solar-powered hats. Keep cool in the sun with a built-in solar fan.
- Solar-powered pest repellent. Keep mosquitoes and rodents away.
- Solar-powered lights for your bike. Be safe while saving the Earth!

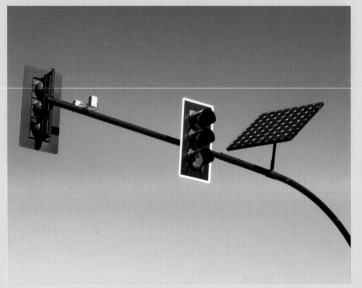

Solar panels have proven to be great energy sources for "smaller" items such as this traffic light, but can they play a larger role in reducing our dependence of fossil fuels?

Solar power has many advantages—the most obvious is that it's free and renewable. Of course, there are drawbacks to solar power. When the Sun isn't shining (like at night or when it's cloudy), you're pretty much out of luck. You can get around this by storing unused solar power in batteries.

Right now, the biggest negative to solar energy is that the photovoltaic cells are expensive and difficult to set up—especially ones that are big enough to generate enough power to run your house. Figure out how much it would cost to set up a solar power system on your house, and how much you pay for electricity every month. How long would it take for the photovoltaic cell to pay for itself?

Explore Further

Take your circuit outdoors on a partly cloudy day. Watch the current reading on the multimeter as the clouds drift across the Sun. How does the current produced from full Sun compare to the current when it's cloudy?

How does the angle that the light hits the photovoltaic cell affect the amount of current produced? Use a protractor to measure the angle of tilt of the photovoltaic cell relative to the light bulb.

How does the color of light affect the photovoltaic cell? Look at red, yellow, and blue light. If you can't find colored filters, you can use colored permanent markers on transparency film. How do other filters, such as sunglasses and windows, affect the current? Change the amount of the photovoltaic cell exposed to light by covering up different areas of the cell with aluminum foil.

How does adding more photovoltaic cells to your circuit affect the amount of current produced? You can hook them up in series (one next to the other) or in parallel (the circuit branches between the first photovoltaic cell to add the second and reconnects on the other side of the first). Which arrangement produces more current?

Methane Madness

Biogas is a funny thing. It's a big part of the global warming problem that can also be part of the solution. Biogas is created by *anaerobic digestion*, or when bacteria, without the presence of oxygen, eat up leaves, dirt, the food in your stomach, and other organic stuff. It's a mixture of methane (the same stuff in natural gas) and carbon dioxide—both big causes of global warming. However, methane can also be used for fuel. Scientists and engineers have been experimenting with different ways of capturing methane in order to meet our energy needs.

JUST THE FACTS

* Methane traps about 21 times more heat in the atmosphere than carbon dioxide.

* Methane stays in the atmosphere for about 12 years.

* There is only about one methane molecule for every 200 carbon dioxide molecules in the atmosphere.

* Landfills create 34% of all methane emissions.

* Methane is released while processing natural gas and coal as well as from gas and manure produced by livestock.

* Wetlands, oceans, and even termites produce methane naturally.

Top right: Cattle farmers in developing countries collect dried cow dung "cakes" and use them as a fuel source. In industrial societies, biogas digesters (pictured above) are being built to process cow manure into energy for use on the farms.

THE EXPERIMENT
How do environmental conditions affect the amount of biogas produced?

Summary

You'll place a bottle of biomass (garbage from plants and animals) in conditions with different amounts of light and heat to find out where the most biogas is produced.

What You Need

- 1 cup (236.6 ml) of soil
- 1 cup (236.6 ml) of manure*
- 1 cup (236.6 ml) of vegetable scraps and grass clippings
- Large bowl
- Mixing spoon
- Funnel
- Measuring cup
- 9 identical plastic water or soda bottles
- 9 large balloons**
- Duct tape
- Measuring tape
- Refrigerator
- Large paper bag

* If you don't have access to farm animals, garden stores sell manure by the bag.

** Don't use water balloons.

Experimental Procedure

1. Dump the soil, manure, and vegetable scraps into a large bowl. Mix them well with the mixing spoon.

2. Use the funnel to pour 1/2 cup of the mixture into each bottle. Shake the bottle gently so it all settles to the bottom.

3. Stretch a deflated balloon over the opening of each bottle. Use the duct tape to tightly seal the balloons onto the bottles.

4. Measure the height of the mixture in the bottle and record it in your lab notebook. Write down the date you made your observation.

5. Place three bottles in the fridge (cold and dark), three in direct sunlight (warm and bright), and three in a large brown paper bag on top of the fridge (warm and dark). Stand the bottles upright. Make sure there's room for the balloons to inflate as the biogas is made. Let everyone in your house know not to disturb the bottles, and put them somewhere your pets can't get at them.

6. Visit the bottles every day for at least two weeks. Measure and write down the level of the mixture in the each bottle. Wrap the measuring tape around each balloon and record its circumference. Make sure you record the date of your observations.

7. When you're done, take the bottles outdoors to remove the balloons. Release the gas away from any flames. Dump the mixture in the bottom of each bottle into a compost pile and recycle the water bottle.

Conclusion

Average the largest balloon circumferences and the level of mixture in the bottles for each location. Make a bar graph of location versus balloon circumference. Large balloons correspond to the greatest production of biogas. Which location had the largest balloons?

What effect do you think light and temperature have on the amount of biogas produced? What would happen if you placed bottles in a cold and bright location?

Make a bar graph of mixture level versus location. Which location had the least amount of mixture in the bottles after two weeks? This corresponds with the most decomposition.

Is there a relationship between the amount of biogas produced and the amount of decomposition?

Take a Closer Look

What makes capturing and burning biogas so great? First of all, it's renewable. As long as we keep producing waste, we'll keep making biogas. And when biogas is burned to create energy, methane is destroyed and kept out of the atmosphere.

Biogas systems are used in rural and developing countries, such as Nepal and Costa Rica, as cheap, easy-to-use energy sources. Cooking and toilet waste is collected, the biogas they release is gathered, and then it's burned. The leftovers from this process can be used as a fertilizer. These systems help save the trees that would otherwise be burned for fuel.

In developed countries such as the United States and Europe, biogas systems or "digesters" are used on some farms to take advantage of all the manure that cows, pigs, and other farm animals create. Digesters help get rid of all that waste (and the smell), and provide energy in the process.

Explore Further

Try different materials in the bottom of the bottles. What combination of soil, manure, and vegetable waste produces the most gas? What combination produces gas the quickest? What's the smallest amount of material you need to make a measurable amount of biogas? Does liquefying the vegetable scraps in a blender or food processor before putting them in the bottles speed up biogas production? What type of manure is best for creating biogas?

Villages in northern India let fresh cow dung dry out for two to five days and then put the cakes in boxes. The boxes are also covered with dung. The dried dung cakes are used primarily as cooking fuel.

Mooo-buuurp!

Which do you think contributes more to global warming: cars or cows?

You might be surprised to learn that cows and other livestock produce more than one-third of the methane released into the atmosphere. That can add up to 50 gallons (189 l) of methane per cow, per day. What's more alarming is that the amount of methane produced by livestock could increase by 60% in 20 years.

But just how do cows and other livestock release this greenhouse gas?

Burps.

That's right, global warming is caused, in part, by cow burps (and to a lesser extent, farts). Scientists are trying to sniff out a solution to this stinky problem. (Yes, cow burps smell.) And while some researchers hope to find a diet that's easier for cattle to digest that will result in less gas, it appears that kangaroos may also hold the key.

Kangaroo gas contains no methane. Special bacteria in kangaroo stomachs eat up all the methane before the gas can be released.

Kangaroos evolved on the plains and deserts of Australia and New Zealand. Their stomachs have had thousands of years to adjust to the grass and other foods they eat, so they have become very efficient at digesting their meals. Special bacteria in the kangaroo's stomach digest the methane, giving kangaroos more energy from the food they eat. Cows, on the other hand, have been imported and exported all over the world. Everywhere they go, they have to get used to new foods—and adjusting to these new foods causes methane-filled gas.

So, to stop global warming all we need to do is inject kangaroo stomach bacteria into every cow on the planet, right?

Unfortunately, it's not that easy. Because the bacteria have evolved to digest Australian and New Zealand grass, the injection may only work for the cows and sheep that eat the same grasses. In the meantime, scientists will have the odorous job of studying the gas of other animals to see if those critters burp methane-free gas.

More Bad News About Cows

Cows also release 64% of the atmosphere's ammonia into the environment, which is a major cause of acid rain.

Consider the land cows need to live on (30% of the Earth's land surface), and the land used to grow their food (another 30% of all farmland). We're talking about a BIG impact here. In the Amazon, about 70% of the rainforest has been cut down to provide grazing land for livestock. Not to mention water pollution from animal poop and all the chemicals that are used (hormones, antibiotics, fertilizer for their feed...). Anyone up for a veggie burger?

Blowing in the Wind

The technology needed to gather energy from the wind has been around for a long time. During the Middle Ages, windmills were used in Iran to grind corn and draw water from wells. In Europe, they ground grain and cereals. Later, windmills were used to power saws and other industrial tools. In the United States, windmills pumped water from deep underground, allowing people to grow crops in many areas where water wasn't easily accessible. Can we put a new spin on this old technology?

The windmills above are hundreds of years old and can be found in the province of La Mancha in central Spain.

JUST THE FACTS

* Wind turbine blades can be anywhere from 9 to 300 feet (3 to 90 m) in diameter.

* Wind needs to blow about 9 miles per hour (15 km per hour) to power a small wind turbine, and at least 13 miles per hour (21 km per hour) to power a wind turbine large enough to create power for electricity companies.

* If the wind blows twice as fast, the windmill will produce eight times as much power.

* About 1% to 2% of the energy coming from the Sun is converted into wind energy— that's about 50 to 100 times more energy than what all the plants on the Earth convert into biomass.

* The Greek inventor Hero made a windmill almost 1,900 years ago. It ran an organ.

THE EXPERIMENT
How does the shape of the blades affect how much electricity a wind turbine produces?

Summary

You'll build a wind turbine and make three sets of different-shaped blades for it. Then you'll measure the voltage produced by each.

What You Need

- Rubber band
- 1.5 volt DC motor*
- Ruler
- Wire cutters
- Insulated wire*
- Electrical tape (optional)
- Voltmeter or multimeter* (see photo on page 23)
- 18 large paper clips
- Scissors
- Thin cardboard**
- Templates on page 40
- Cork
- Masking tape
- Fan
- Marker

* You can find these supplies at an electronics store.

** You can use a cereal box.

Make the Wind Turbine

1. Use the rubber band to attach the body of the motor to the end of the ruler. Be sure the shaft of the motor extends beyond the end of the ruler. The motor's leads or outlets will point toward the other end of the ruler.

2. Use the wire cutters to cut two 12-inch (30-cm) pieces of insulated wire. Then remove about 1 inch (2.5 cm) of the insulation from each end of both wires.

3. Attach one end of each wire to one of the motor's leads or outlets. Secure the wires with electrical tape if needed.

4. Tape the middle of the wires to the ruler to hold them in place. Attach the other ends of the wires to the voltmeter. (The voltmeter will measure how much voltage your windmill produces.) Now you're ready to build the blades for your turbine!

5. Use the scissors and the template labeled A to cut out six pieces of cardboard. These will be the first set of windmill blades.

6. Straighten out the bottom end of each of the paper clips. Tape each cardboard piece to the middle of a paper clip to make a windmill blade. The long end of the paper clip should stick out.

7. Stick the six windmill blades into the cork about ¼ inch (5 mm) from the end. Space them equally around the cork.

8. Repeat steps 5 through 7, creating two more sets of windmill blades using the remaining two templates (B and C). Each blade shape has the same surface area.

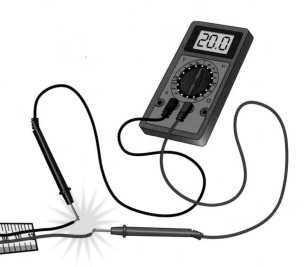

Experimental Procedure

1. Insert the motor's shaft through the center of the cork. The blades should be at the far end of the cork, away from the motor. Make sure the shaft goes through the center of the cork, so the windmill doesn't wobble when it spins. Place the turbine at least 1 foot (30. 5 cm) in front of a fan. Use a piece of tape to mark the position of the windmill and the fan. They'll need to be in the same place throughout the experiment.

2. Now you're going to figure out the best angle for the blades. Twist the blades so they're perpendicular to the end of the cork. (Looking at the end of the cork, you'll see the narrow edge of the blades.) Turn on the fan. If the blades don't spin, turn them a tiny bit so that they're slightly tilted.

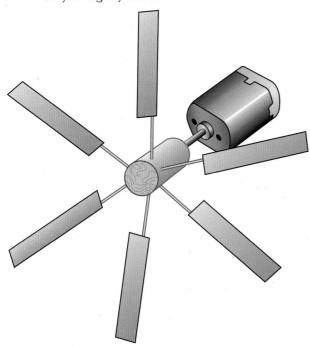

3. Repeat step 2, tilting the blades in small increments until the blades start spinning. When the blades start spinning, measure the voltage produced. If you need to, adjust the settings on the voltmeter until it shows a voltage reading.

4. Keep tilting the blades of the turbine until you find the angle that produces the greatest voltage. Record this voltage.

5. Test the voltage at least four more times. Record the voltage each time.

6. Use the marker to mark the angle of the blades directly on the cork. Just draw a short, straight line beneath each blade. The line should line up with the angle of the blade.

7. Now you're ready to test the other blade shapes. Remove the first set of blades and insert the longer rectangular blades. Turn the blades so that they line up with the marks you made on the cork in step 6. The second set of blades should be at the same angle as the first ones.

8. Place the turbine in front of the fan, making sure that both are in the same places as they were in step 2. Turn on the fan and record the voltage produced.

9. Repeat step 8 at least four more times and record the voltage each time.

10. Repeat steps 7 through 9 with the trapezoid-shaped blades.

Conclusion

Average the voltage for each blade shape. Make a bar graph of blade shape versus voltage. Which shape produced the highest voltage? What other changes could you make to that shape to increase the voltage even more?

Take a Closer Look

Anything that moves, including air, uses energy to move. Energy of motion is called *kinetic energy*. Wind turbines take the kinetic energy out of the wind and convert it to electrical energy. Then we can use the electrical energy to light and heat our homes. There are two basic types of wind electric turbines: *vertical-axis* (these look kind of like egg-beaters), and *horizontal-axis* (these look like airplane propellers).

Horizontal-axis wind turbines are most common.

Each wind turbine has these parts:

- Rotor or blades, which convert the wind's kinetic energy into rotational kinetic energy.

- *Nacelle* or the housing for the drive train along with a gearbox and a generator. (These are the parts that convert the rotational kinetic energy of the rotor into electricity, just like the motor in this experiment.)

- Tower, which supports the rotor and other parts.

Wind energy has many benefits. Most importantly, it doesn't produce any greenhouse gases while creating electricity. And of course, you can never "use up" the wind, which makes it a renewable energy source.

If wind energy were to provide 20% of our electricity, it could get rid of one-third or more of the greenhouse gas emissions from fossil-fuel power plants.

Where Does Wind Come From?

Wind is actually created by the Sun. Water and land absorb heat from the Sun at different rates. This causes parts of the atmosphere to heat differently, too. The hot air in the atmosphere rises, and then cooler air rushes in to replace it. All the air moving around is wind.

*Explore*Further

Look at other blade properties and how they affect voltage and windmill spin speed. Try changing the number, angle, spacing, size, shape, or the material you use (cardboard, plastic, etc.) to make the blades. You can also investigate the effect of wind speed on voltage and spin rate.

Try making a vertical wind turbine and compare its performance to the horizontal turbines used here.

Construct a simple wind tunnel using a cardboard box to reduce variations in airflow. Use a long box (or tape two shorter boxes together) that is open at two ends. Place the fan at one end and your turbine inside the box.

Templates for Fan Blades

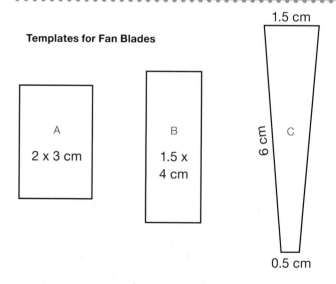

A
2 x 3 cm

B
1.5 x 4 cm

1.5 cm

6 cm   C

0.5 cm

Putting the Sun to Work

Sunlight is a great heater, and you can use it to help heat your home. The only problem is that it doesn't come with an on/off switch. To make the Sun work for you, you have to be smart about when to let the sunlight in and when to keep it out. This takes some planning and ingenuity, but past civilizations had a better handle on this passive solar heating than we do today—mainly because it's the only heat they had.

JUST THE FACTS

* 49% of the radiation from the Sun reaches the Earth as heat instead of visible light.

* During winter in the Northern Hemisphere, the Sun spends each day in the southern part of the sky. In the Southern Hemisphere, the winter Sun is in the northern part.

* The amount of solar energy that reaches the Earth's surface every year is 29,000 times greater than the amount of energy used in the United States.

* With proper design, you can rely on solar radiation for 20% to 80% of the heat you need in the winter. That's how much energy can enter from windows and doors on the equator-facing side of your house.

Before air conditioning and indoor heating, where and how you built your house could be the difference between life and death.

THE EXPERIMENT
How does the direction your house faces affect the amount of heat it absorbs from the Sun?

Summary

You'll build four identical model houses out of shoeboxes. Then you'll set them in the Sun, oriented in different directions, and monitor the temperature inside and outside the "houses."

What You Need

- 4 identical shoeboxes
- Scissors
- Ruler
- Tape
- Plastic wrap
- A few sunny afternoons
- Compass
- 5 outdoor thermometers, small enough to fit in the shoeboxes

Experimental Procedure

1. On a long side of one of the shoeboxes, use the scissors to cut two windows. The windows should be the same size and centered between the top and bottom and both edges of the long side. Carefully measure the size and position of the windows and make identical windows on the other three shoeboxes.

2. Tape plastic wrap over the holes in all of the boxes. This will serve as the panes in the windows. Make sure you tape all around the outside of the plastic wrap so there's no airflow.

3. On a sunny afternoon, find a flat spot outside to put your shoeboxes. Make sure the boxes aren't on a hill, there's no shade, and they're all on the same type of surface (for instance, all on grass or all on concrete). Use the compass to find north. Place the first box with its windows facing due north. Use the compass to face the windows on the other boxes south, east, and west. Label the boxes with the direction their windows face.

4. Put a thermometer in the middle of each box. Put the remaining thermometer on the ground between the boxes. Wait five minutes, and then write down the temperature of each thermometer in your lab book. (You should be able to see the thermometer through the windows. If not, open the box briefly to read the temperature.) This is your starting temperature.

5. Record the temperature of each thermometer every 10 minutes for at least three hours. Make sure none of the boxes are shaded during the entire experiment.

6. Repeat steps 3 to 5 on at least two other sunny afternoons. Put the boxes in the same location at the same time of day as you did on the first day.

Conclusion

Make line graphs of temperature versus time for each box and each trial. You can put all the data from one afternoon on a single graph if you use a different colored line for each box. What do the lines look like? Does the temperature change slowly or quickly? Group the graphs by the directions the boxes faced. Do you see any common patterns? What other factors, besides direction, could influence the shape of the graphs?

Calculate the change in temperature for each box and each trial by subtracting the starting temperature from the ending temperature. Average the change in temperature for each direction. Which direction had the greatest change in temperature and which had the least? How did the temperature changes inside the boxes compare to the temperature changes outside?

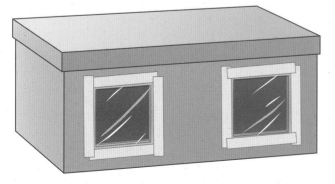

Take a Closer Look

Passive solar building takes advantage of the Sun's power to heat and cool your home without using electrical or mechanical systems. These ideas aren't new. In ancient Greece, Aristotle and Socrates described how houses should face south and shelter the north sides from winter winds. Later, the Romans improved on these ideas by using windowpanes to hold in the heat. Houses were built to use the Sun until the 1900s when heating systems (powered by gas and oil) became cheap and easy to install. Now that the price of fuel is rising and these heating systems aren't so cheap, architects and builders are taking advantage of passive solar design again.

There are three ways that a house can be designed to use the Sun's heat:

• Direct solar gain uses windows, shutters, and overhang to control the amount of sunlight that gets into the house.

• Indirect solar gain captures the heat from sunlight by using a big mass, such as a water tank or solid concrete wall, to store the heat during the day and give it off at night.

• Isolated solar gain captures the Sun's heat and moves it into or out of the building using water or air.

What effect does the time of year or season have on the impact of direction on the heating of your house? Does the direction your house faces in the summer matter as much as it does in the winter? What if you live in a very warm climate? How should you orient your house to keep it cooler?

Shutters closed against the midday Sun allow air to circulate while tempering the effect of the Sun's intense rays.

*Explore*Further

How can you modify your model houses to heat up even more in the sunlight? Try painting the outside and inside of the boxes, adding roofing material, modifying the size, shape, location, and material of the windows. You can even change the color of the windows.

Investigate how well your model houses stay warm after the Sun has set. After measuring the temperature as your model houses heat up, move them into the shade and continue to record temperatures to see how quickly they cool back down. You could even leave the model houses where they are and measure the temperature every 30 minutes over an entire day.

You can also experiment with different methods for keeping the houses the same temperature all day long. Use dark, heavy materials, such as stone, to make the floor in your house. The stone soaks up the heat during the day and slowly releases it at night. Try tiles, too. Or, make one entire long side of your shoebox into a plastic wrap window. Cut a piece of wood the same size as that window, paint it black, and place it inside the box 1 inch (2.5 cm) behind the window. The wall will soak up heat during the day, keeping the insides fairly cool, and then release the heat into the house after dark.

take action

You can take advantage of these passive solar building ideas without tearing down your house and building a new one.

Plant trees. Plant deciduous trees and bushes near the side of your house that faces the equator (south in the Northern Hemisphere and north in the Southern Hemisphere). The leaves will keep the house shady in the hot summer. In the winter, they'll lose their leaves so the Sun can get inside your house and warm it up.

Paint your house. The color of your house can reflect or absorb heat from the Sun. First figure out if you spend more energy heating your house in the winter or cooling it in the summer. If you run your heater more, paint your house a darker color so it can absorb the Sun's heat better. If cooling your house in the summer takes more energy, paint your house a lighter shade to reflect the heat.

Hang curtains. In the winter, keep the windows facing the equator unblocked during the day and close them up tight with heavy curtains at night to keep in that warm air. In the summer, keep the curtains and windows closed during the heat of the day. Open them up when it starts cooling off at night.

People Power

We can harvest alternative energies from the Sun, wind, water, plants, and decomposing matter, but what about people? An average-sized person stores as much energy in fat as a 2,000-pound (900 kg) battery. A lot of people spend time exercising, burning up the energy (calories) stored in that fat. What if we could harness all those burned calories and turn them into electricity?

Scientists are working on ways to harvest human energy. Here are some cutting-edge technologies that harvest people power.

Crowd Farm

Every time you take a step, the energy that goes into the floor when your foot hits it could power a 60-watt light bulb for a second. That may not sound like much, but can you imagine harnessing the energy of a whole crowd of people walking around? Students at the Massachusetts Institute of Technology (MIT) did. They designed a floor to put in train stations and other places where a lot of people walk. The floor has just a little give to it so that it slides around as people walk. This sliding motion is converted into electricity. When a crowd takes at 30,000 steps, it generates enough energy to power a moving train for one second.

Energy Harvesting Knee Brace

The Biomechanical Energy Harvester is a knee brace that converts the swing of your leg into electricity. With a brace on each leg, you can generate up to 5 watts of energy. If you really get moving, you can generate up to 13 watts. If you hook the knee braces up to your cell phone, you can generate enough energy to power your cell phone for 30 minutes with only one minute of walking.

Hydroelectric Shoes

What if you could put a water wheel inside your shoe? That's exactly what Robert Komarechka, a Canadian inventor, did. His hydro-powered shoe has a tiny water wheel inside the sole. There are water sacs under the heel and ball of the foot. As you walk, the water flows between the two sacs, back and forth with each step. In between is a tiny turbine and generator that converts the energy from the moving water into electricity.

Battery Backpacks

Think your school backpack is heavy? Soldiers carry 80 pounds (36 kg) of equipment in their backpacks, plus another 20 pounds (9 kg) of spare batteries to power all their gadgets like radios and night vision goggles. The military is looking into technology that will convert the energy the soldiers generate carrying the backpacks into energy they can use to power their equipment. In one design, a sack is suspended from the backpack. As you walk, the sack bounces up and down on springs. A small generator inside the sack converts the bounce into electricity. Another model harnesses the energy generated when the straps on the backpack stretch and rub against your back as you move. The newest version of the backpack shown below can generate up to 20 watts when walking and 25 watts when running. (A cell phone only uses .5 watt.)

Dr. Larry Rome, the inventor of the Suspended-load Backpack, shows off a prototype.

Out the Window

Opening your windows while the air conditioner is running isn't going to cool off the planet—or your house. Most of the energy used by your house each month is for heating and cooling. And a big chunk of that energy goes right out your windows, literally. Heat still moves through a closed window, and it moves through a window much faster than it moves through a wall. Short of boarding up all your windows, what can you do to reduce the amount of energy you use to keep your house cool in the summer and warm in the winter?

JUST THE FACTS

* 1 square foot (0.1 m) of window can lose as much heat as 10 square feet (3 m) of wall.

* A $1/16$-inch (1.6 mm) crack around a 3- by 5-foot (0.9 by 1.5 m) window is the equivalent of a 10-inch (25 cm) diameter hole in your wall. (That's a hole about the size of this book!)

* Installing double-paned windows can reduce heating costs by 25%.

* In the United States, 50% of the energy people use in their homes is used for heating and cooling. (If you count heating water, too, the number goes up to 75%.)

* Up to 40% of the energy used in German homes goes to heating, including heating water.

THE EXPERIMENT
How does adding another pane of glass to a window affect how much heat escapes?

Summary

You'll use a CD case to make a single- and double-paned window. Then you'll shine a lamp on each type of window and measure the temperature on both sides to see how much heat is transmitted through the window.

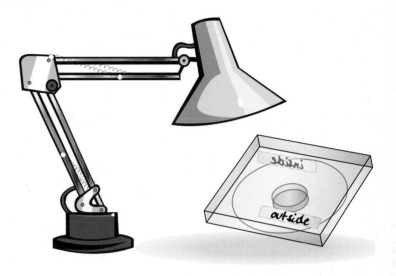

What You Need

- Clear CD case, 1 cm (0.4 inches) thick
- Clear packing tape
- Permanent marker and tape
- Thermometer
- Gooseneck lamp with a 60-watt light bulb
- Ruler
- Helper
- Stopwatch

Experimental Procedure

1. Remove the black plastic insert from the CD case. Use the clear packing tape to seal the hole in the CD case near the hinge. You don't want any air flowing in and out of the case. The closed CD case represents a double-paned window.

2. In one corner of the case, use the permanent marker and tape to mark one side "inside" and the other "outside."

3. Let the thermometer and CD case sit in the room for five minutes. Write down the room temperature from your thermometer in your lab book.

4. Turn on the lamp. Use the ruler to hold the CD case 2 inches (5 cm) away from the light bulb. Make sure the side marked "outside" is facing the light bulb. This simulates the bright Sun shining on the window. Hold the CD in place for two minutes. Have your helper time you with the stopwatch.

5. After two minutes, turn off the light and place the thermometer against the "outside" of the CD case, right in the center. The temperature will rise as you watch. Record the highest temperature in your lab notebook.

6. Let the thermometer and case cool back down to room temperature. This should take about five minutes.

7. Repeat steps 4 through 6, measuring the temperature of the "inside" of the case (the part that faces away from the light bulb). This represents the inside of the window on a bright sunny day.

8. Repeat steps 4 through 7 at least five more times. You should have six sets of measurements for both the inside and outside of your double-paned window.

9. Carefully remove the packing tape and separate the two pieces of the CD case. Set one piece aside. Now you have a single-paned window.

10. Repeat steps 2 through 8, testing the heat transference of your single-paned window.

Conclusion

To find out how much the temperatures of the inside and outside of the windows changed, subtract the room temperature from all the temperature readings you recorded.

Average the change in temperature for the inside of your double-paned window. Then average the change in temperature for the outside of the double-paned window. How do they compare?

Average the change in temperature for the inside of your single-paned window. Then average the change in temperature for the outside of the single-paned window. How do they compare?

Which window had the biggest difference between inside and outside temperature? Which had the smallest? Which window would you use if you wanted to keep the inside of your home cool on a sunny day?

Take a Closer Look

Heat moved through the CD case the same way it moves through a window, by *radiation* and *conduction*. Radiation is the transfer of heat through light (or electromagnetic waves). Conduction is the transfer of heat by direct contact between the molecules in the air and window. Radiation from the Sun heats the air outside the window and inside the window. Conduction happens when the window warms up and the heat moves through the window.

In the summer, when it's warmer outside than it is inside, windows conduct heat from the outside in, warming up the inside of your house. In the winter, when it's warmer inside than it is outside, windows conduct heat from the inside out, cooling the inside of your house. This is exactly opposite of what you want. When you add a pane to your window, you're sandwiching air in between two pieces of glass. This layer of air acts like insulation, slowing down the rate of heat transference.

People who make windows use the U-value to measure how well a window conducts heat. The U-value is the number of watts of energy that will be lost per square meter at a certain temperature. The higher the U-value, the more heat will pass through the window. For example, a single-paned glass window has a U-value of 1, but a double-paned window has a U-value of $\frac{1}{2}$, which means it loses half as much energy. Snow has a U-value of 1, so it insulates as well as a single pane of glass. Cardboard has a U-value of $\frac{1}{3}$, which means its insulates better than a window. Surprisingly, still air is the best insulator of all—it has a U-value of $\frac{1}{5}$. That's what makes a double-paned window insulate so well.

*Explore*Further

How does the distance between the panes affect the change in temperature? What about the size of the panes? What if you used three or four panes in your window? How do different types of curtains or blinds affect the amount of heat that gets through the windows?

Some windows with more than one pane are filled with gases, such as carbon dioxide or argon. Put a tiny bit of baking soda and vinegar (less than a teaspoon [0.5 ml] of each) in the deeper half of the CD case. Then close it quickly. The case will fill with carbon dioxide. How does this affect the difference in temperature between the inside and outside?

Design an experiment to measure how well single- and double-paned windows keep the cold out of your home. Use a protractor to investigate how the angle at which the light hits the window affects the temperature difference between the inside and outside of a window.

rethinking **Garbage**

The average person in the United States throws away 4 pounds (1.8 kg) of garbage a day. Over a year, that's the equivalent of throwing a rhinoceros in the trash.

Archeologists spend a lot of time sifting through the trash of ancient civilizations. Mostly they find broken pots, tools, and bones. What will future archeologists find when they look at our landfills?

To get a good idea, look in your garbage can. You might find everything from packaging, food scraps, and grass clippings to old toys, orphan socks, and foam packaging.

But trash in landfills doesn't just come from our homes. It also comes from everywhere else people throw things away, like schools, restaurants, stores, and hospitals.

So where does all this paper, glass, plastic, and metal come from? If we look at the contents of landfills by category, we get a different picture of what we throw away. One-third of the trash in landfills come from containers and packaging. Food scraps and yard trimmings make up one-quarter of our trash. The rest is split between durable and nondurable goods. Durable goods include appliances such as refrigerators, ovens, and computers, as well as mattresses and furniture. Nondurable goods are things that are used for fewer than three years, such as clothes, newspapers, and toys.

How about what's NOT in our landfills?

In the past few decades, we've become pretty good at recycling. About half of our steel, aluminum cans, paper, and yard trimmings are recycled or composted. And about one-third of plastic bottles, glass, and even tires are recycled. In fact, 82 million tons (74 million kg) of trash is recycled at landfills. That saves us the energy equivalent of 10 billion gallons (38 billion liters) of gasoline.

The projects in this chapter examine how we can reduce the amount of garbage we make. You can explore ways to reduce the amount of trash your family generates. Try recycling and buying less packaging, and find out how well biodegradable products work.

Garbage Diet

Garbage stinks. Yet, no matter how much we hate it, we keep making it. People have been trying to figure out what to do about garbage for a long time. Archeologists digging up sites at 12,000-year-old settlements in Israel have found thousands of pieces of garbage isolated in two buildings. These might be the first dumps. During the 1700s, New York City employed hogs as the first garbage disposals. Because there were no garbage trucks or city dumps, people threw their trash out of their homes into the street. Hogs roamed the streets, eating the garbage.

Can you reduce the amount of garbage your family sends to the landfill? Turn your science fair experiment into a family project to see if you can use recycling to reduce your refuse.

JUST THE FACTS

* Throughout the world, urban residents generate up to three times as much solid waste as rural residents.

* The greater a family's income, the more waste they create. On average, high-income households dispose double the trash of middle-income households, and four or more times the amount of low-income households.

* The United States is the world's top trasher, throwing away twice the average of most other industrialized countries.

* The United States has nearly tripled its trash production since 1960. Thirty-two percent of the trash is recovered and recycled or composted, 14% is burned at combustion facilities, and the remaining 54% is put in landfills.

* In 2005, recycling prevented the release of approximately 49 million tons (44 billion kg) of carbon into the air.

* 49 million tons (44 billion kg) of carbon is roughly the amount emitted annually by 39 million cars—so recycling saves the energy equivalent of 11 billion gallons (42 billion liters) of gasoline.

Summary

You'll measure how much garbage your family produces. Then you'll spend a month trying to reduce this amount by recycling.

What You Need

- Large plastic garbage bags
- Permanent marker
- Gallon-sized (3.8 l), self-sealing plastic bags
- Latex gloves
- Scale

Experimental Procedure

1. Get your whole family involved! For the first week, place two garbage bags in the kitchen. Use the permanent marker to label one bag "food items," and the other one "dry garbage." Your family will put all their garbage into these bags for the first week of the experiment.

2. Give each member of your family two gallon-sized (3.8 l), self-sealing plastic bags: one is for food, the other is for dry garbage. It's very important that your family members place ALL the garbage they would normally throw away outside the home (at work, school, etc.) in the bags. (This includes leftover lunch and soda bottles, but doesn't include tissues and toilet paper.) When you get home, collect their garbage and put it in the bigger bags. Wash out the smaller bags every night for them, and have them reuse the bags the next day. (Hey, it's the least you can do.)

3. After the week of garbage collecting, weigh yourself and record your weight. Then weigh yourself holding the dry garbage bag. Subtract your weight from this number. That's how many pounds of dry garbage your family produced. Do the same thing for the food garbage bag. Add the weight of the two garbage bags together to find the total amount of garbage your family produces in one week.

4. Put on the latex gloves and go through the garbage with your family. Can you recycle or compost most of your garbage? Devise a plan and implement it. (See the Take Action section for ideas.)

5. Continue to collect your family's garbage and weigh it at the end of every week for three weeks.

Conclusion

How much did your total garbage decrease? Make a line graph of time in weeks versus total amount of trash. Which type of garbage decreased the most—dry garbage or food garbage? Which was easier to reduce? How much garbage did you keep out of the landfill during your experiment?

Take a Closer Look

You probably only think about the trash when you have to take it to the curb on trash pick-up day. A big truck comes to haul it away and you forget all about it. Where exactly does all that garbage go? Most of it is buried in landfills. Some gets recycled or recovered and some is burned.

There are two ways to bury trash. A dump is an open hole in which

trash is dumped and buried. A landfill is built into or on top of the ground. It's carefully designed so that trash is isolated from the surrounding environment (groundwater, air, rain) with a bottom liner and daily covering of soil. Many modern landfills also have *leachate* and methane collection systems. Leachate is water that has percolated through the landfill and contains contaminated substances. Methane, a greenhouse gas, is produced as the trash decomposes. (Often the methane is pumped to a power plant where it can be burned as fuel.)

While landfills protect the environment from pollution, the trash does not decompose much. A landfill is designed just to bury trash so there is little of the water or oxygen that bacteria need to decompose the garbage. Once a landfill closes, the site must be maintained and monitored for up to 30 years.

Explore Further

After the first week, when you have your "base amount" of garbage, add some more bags for paper, plastic, and other recyclable materials. Keep track of how much garbage moves out of the garbage bags and into the recycle bags.

Talk your friends and neighbors into participating in the experiment. Make it a contest—who can reduce their garbage the most?

Reduce It

Reducing garbage starts when you buy the stuff you'll eventually throw away. Ask yourself these four questions before buying something:

- **Can I reuse it?** Choose cloth grocery bags, rechargeable batteries, and containers that you can use to hold different stuff.
- **Will it last?** Is the product well made or will it break easily?
- **How much packaging does it have?** Buy things you use a lot in big containers and avoid things with lots of extra packaging.
- **Do I really need it?** Are you just going to throw it away next week or next month? Rent or borrow things you only need for a short time.

take action

Here are some basic tips for reducing the amount of trash you throw away.

Recycle, recycle, recycle!

A lot of garbage is paper and plastic containers that can be reused (such as scrap paper or water bottles) and then recycled. Contact your local recycling service and landfill to find out exactly what materials can be recycled. You might be surprised.

In the kitchen

Use cloth kitchen towels and napkins. Reuse plastic food containers for leftovers instead of aluminum foil or plastic wrap.

Junk the junk mail

Remove your family from catalog and other junk mail lists. Encourage your parents to sign up for online bill paying. This reduces the paper sent every month, the return envelopes and all the inserts, not to mention the paper check.

Bring your own

If your parents, teachers, or neighbors buy coffee in the morning, get them in the habit of bringing a travel mug instead of relying on a new paper cup every day. Most places even offer a discount if you bring your own. While you're at it, consider patronizing establishments that don't use polystyrene foam for their "to go" products.

Paper or plastic?

Bring your own tote bags to the grocery store, so you won't have to choose between paper or plastic. Plastic grocery bags have created one of the biggest litter problems in the world.

Recharge

Next time your game batteries run out, be sure to dispose of them properly. Then, convince your parents to invest in rechargeable batteries for all your household gadgets.

At school

Bring a lunch box, and challenge your classmates to come to school with waste-free lunches. Also, set up a location in your classroom for used binders, pencils, folders, and even lunch boxes and backpacks that your family no longer needs and are still in good shape. Maybe you can even set up a classroom swap—trade your clothes, video games, books, and more. Convince your school to provide more recycling bins, and make sure everyone knows how to use them.

Compost

Start a compost bin in the backyard for food scraps and leftovers. (See page 63.)

Bottle it yourself

Get yourself a good quality reusable bottle that you can refill with your favorite beverage or water and take it with you. Avoid individual serving containers.

Flip it

Use both sides of a sheet of paper before recycling it. Also, use scrap paper for art projects. If your parents work at an office that uses lots of paper, ask them to bring some home for your drawing and craft projects.

Make it easy

Make recycling convenient for yourself, your family, and others. For example, if your family spends a lot of time in the car, make sure you keep a bag just for recycled materials in the back of the car.

Recycled Paper

You probably put your leftover paper in a bin and send it to the recycling center. And that's a really good start, but do you try to use the paper that's made out of these leftovers? Some people think that recycled paper isn't as good as paper that's made brand new, so they don't buy it. Is there a difference between recycled and new paper? Can you tell that this book was printed on recycled paper?

JUST THE FACTS

* One tree filters up to 60 pounds (27 kg) of pollutants from the air every year.

* Recycling paper uses 60% less energy than manufacturing paper from new wood.

* In the United States, each person consumes more than 690 pounds (313 kg) of paper each year. That's twice as much as the average Australian and 313 times as much as someone in Vietnam. Japan and Hong Kong are a distant second and third to the US, with 496 pounds (225 kg) and 485 pounds (220 kg) per person, respectively.

* One ton of paper made from recycled paper instead of new wood saves 7,000 gallons (30,000 l) of water, 20 trees, 60 pounds (30 kg) of air pollutants, and 4,000 kilowatt hours of electricity. (That's enough to run a three-bedroom house for one year!)

THE EXPERIMENT
How does the type of paper (new or recycled) affect its strength?

Summary

You'll add weight to samples of new and recycled paper until they break. You'll use your measurements to calculate the "breaking length" of each type of paper, which will tell you how strong the paper is.

What You Need

- Ruler
- 1 sheet of new notebook paper
- Food scale
- Scissors
- Duct tape
- Table with thick, flat edge
- Light plastic bucket with handle
- Approximately 2,000 pennies* (or other small, heavy objects that each weigh the same amount)
- 1 sheet of recycled notebook paper

* If you don't have $20 worth of pennies, ask a bank to exchange a $20 bill

Experimental Procedure

1. Use the ruler to measure the length and width of the new paper in centimeters. (Measuring in metrics will make the math a lot easier.) Multiply these measurements together to get the area of the paper in centimeters squared (cm^2). Then divide this by 10,000 to convert the area to meters squared (m^2). Be sure to write all of this in your lab notebook.

2. Carefully weigh the sheet of paper on the scale in grams. If your scale isn't sensitive enough to weigh one sheet of paper, put 20 pieces of paper on the scale and then divide the weight by 20 to get the weight of one sheet.

3. Cut a 5 mm-wide strip down the long side of your piece of paper. Do not wrinkle or tear the strip. Try to make the edges as smooth as possible.

4. Tear off a 10 cm-long piece of duct tape. Use it to tape at least 3 cm of one end of the paper strip to the table edge. The strip should hang straight down.

5. Tear off a 20 cm-long piece of duct tape. You'll use this piece to attach the bucket to the bottom of the paper strip. The tape should loop around the bucket handle and then sandwich the bottom part of the paper strip. At least 3 cm of the tape should stick to the front and back of the paper strip.

6. Add one penny at a time to the bucket until the paper breaks. If the paper slips out from the tape instead of just ripping, go back to step 3 and start over with a new strip of paper.

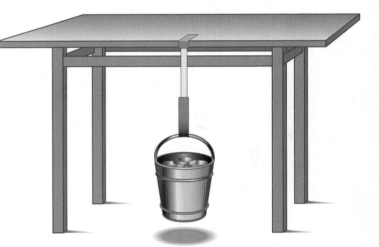

7. When the paper breaks, remove the duct tape from the bucket. Collect any pennies that fell out and put them back in the bucket. Weigh the bucket and pennies. Record their weight in grams and write it down in your lab notebook.

8. Measure the width of the paper where it broke and write it down in your lab notebook.

9. Repeat steps 3 through 8 at least four more times. Average the weights of the bucket.

10. Repeat steps 1 through 9 using the recycled paper.

Conclusion

For each type of paper, figure out how much mass the paper has for a square meter. To do this, divide the weight of one piece of paper (from step 2) by its area (from step 1). This is the paper's basis weight. Then average the weight of the bucket of pennies it took to break each type of paper.

A paper's strength is measured by its breaking length. The breaking length is how long the paper can be before it will break under its own weight. To calculate the paper's breaking length, you'll need:

• The basis weight (bw). (You just calculated this.)

• The average mass (weight) of the pennies and bucket that broke the paper. (We'll call this m^b because it's the *mass* that *broke* the paper).

• The width of the paper where it broke (W) in meters. You measured W in step 8.

To calculate the breaking length, you'll use this equation:

$$\text{Breaking length} = m_b / (W \times bw)$$

First, multiply the W (width of the paper) and the bw (basis weight). Then divide the mb by the number you just calculated.

For example:

If your paper has a basis weight of 20 g/m^2, a breaking width of 0.0005 m (or 5 mm), and it took 450 g (about 1 pound) to break the paper, the breaking length would be:

$$450 \text{ g}/(.0005 \text{ m} \times 20 \text{ g/m}^2) = 45,000 \text{ m}$$

This means that if you had a piece of paper 45,000 meters (28 miles) long or longer, the paper would break under its own weight. The longer the breaking length, the stronger the paper.

How does the breaking length of the new paper compare to the recycled paper? How about other properties of the paper, such as texture (how it feels) or color? Try giving a sheet of each kind of paper to some friends and see if they can tell the difference.

Take a Closer Look

New paper is made from trees grown specifically to make paper. Every part of the tree is used in the papermaking process. The bark and roots are burned to provide energy for the mill. The wood is chopped up for *pulping*, a chemical process that separates the wood fibers from other wood parts. The pulp is treated with bleach and other chemicals to create the right color. Then it's rolled out, dried, and cut into paper.

Recycled paper is made from recovered paper. First, the recovered paper must be sorted, cleaned, and de-inked. Then the recovered paper is pulped, taking the place of chopped wood. After that, the same process used to make new paper is used to make recycled paper.

Paper can't be recycled over and over again. Eventually the fibers become too weak and short to be used again. That's why new paper fiber is usually mixed in with recycled paper when it's turned into paper products. Recycled paper products usually say what percentage of *post-consumer waste* paper they contain. Post-consumer waste means that someone (like you) used the paper and then recycled it.

Explore **Further**

Test other types of paper such as paper towels, copy paper, newspaper, magazine paper, coffee filters, construction paper, and wax paper. How do the strengths of all these compare? How do the strengths of the recycled versions of these paper products compare to the products made from new paper?

After setting up the experiment, use a paintbrush to coat the paper with water or oil. How does this affect your results?

Is Bulk Better?

So, the first of the three Rs is "reduce," right? That means buying a little bit of stuff is better for the environment than buying a lot of stuff. Well, actually, it's not always better to buy less stuff. Sometimes when you think you're buying less stuff, you're actually buying more. That's because of the packaging. There are very few things you can buy at a store without some sort of packaging. Even produce at the grocery store usually has a little sticker on it. Most of this packaging ends up in a landfill. What can you do to reduce the amount of packaging you use in the first place?

JUST THE FACTS

* A 4-ounce (100 ml) yogurt container generates 74% more waste than a 32-ounce (946 ml) container.

* About one-third of the waste from the average household is from packaging.

* About one-third of packaging is plastic, one-third is paper, and the rest is glass and metal.

* Many countries have no requirement for how much or what type of "recycled" content is in a product labeled "recycled." When making a purchase, look for a product with the highest stated amount of "post-consumer content." That means it was made from materials that would otherwise be buried in a landfill.

THE EXPERIMENT
How does the size of a product affect the amount of packaging used?

Summary

You'll purchase several different sizes of the same cereal, and then compare the amount of cereal in the package to the amount of packaging.

What You Need

- Scale
- 3 or more different-sized containers of the same type of cereal*
- Bowl or bag

* The cereal should be the same type, but doesn't need to be the same brand. The packaging can also be different (boxes vs. bags).

Experimental Procedure

1. Weigh the smallest box of cereal before you open it. Write this in your lab notebook.

2. Pour the cereal into a bowl or bag so that you can eat it later.

3. Now weigh just the cereal box by itself in ounces (or grams). (This will make it easier to do the math later!) Be sure to include the bag inside the box and any bits of paper that came off when you opened the box. Write the weight of the packaging in your lab notebook.

4. Subtract the weight of the full box from the weight of the packaging to get the weight of just the cereal. Write the weight of the cereal in your lab notebook.

5. Divide the weight of the packaging by the weight of the cereal. This is how much packaging 1 ounce (28.3 g) of cereal uses. Write down this number, too.

6. Repeat steps 1 through 5 for the rest of the cereal containers.

7. Eat the cereal. Don't forget to recycle the boxes.

Conclusion

Make a bar graph of box size versus the amount of packaging per ounce of cereal (from step 5). Which size box had the least amount of packaging per ounce of cereal? Which had the most?

To see how the amount of packaging relates to the price of the cereal, divide the price of each cereal by its weight in ounces. This will tell you how much 1 ounce (28.3 g) of cereal costs. Create a bar graph of box size versus cost per ounce of cereal. Which size box cost the least per ounce of cereal? Which cost the most? How much do you think you're paying for packaging?

Compare the packaging per ounce of cereal to the cost per ounce of cereal. How does the amount of packaging relate to the cost? Which size (if any) gives the lowest price and the least amount of packaging? Which size box do you recommend?

Take a Closer Look

Engineers and designers create the containers and labels for just about everything you buy. Packaging needs to keep the item from breaking, hold it together, keep it clean and fresh, meet lots of legal regulations, provide information about the product, make it easy to transport and, of course, make it look good so you'll buy it.

There are actually three different levels of packaging.

Primary packaging is what you see when you go to the store, such as the actual box that the cereal is in, the jar that holds the peanut butter, or the carton for the eggs.

The containers of cereal, peanut butter, and eggs were all put in some other container (usually a box) and maybe even shrink wrapped with plastic so it

could be transported to the store. This is called the **secondary packaging**.

And there may have been even more packaging on top of that! **Tertiary packaging** is the even bigger boxes, crates, barrels, and other containers along with any cushioning and insulating materials (like foam peanuts and bubble wrap) that are used to transport the cereal, peanut butter, and eggs from the manufacturing plant (or farm) to the distribution center where they're loaded into trucks and delivered to the store.

That's a lot more packaging for cereal than just the box you bought. And don't forget about the very last layer of packaging you added to the box of cereal— the grocery bag you carried it home in.

Explore Further

Investigate the amount of packaging other products use. Try spaghetti sauce, laundry detergent, crackers, candy, milk, juice, and shampoo. Do any of the packaging materials contain recycled materials?

Contact your grocery store and see if you can watch when the next delivery truck brings in a load of food. Write down the secondary and tertiary packaging (see Take a Closer Look) that you see. Is any of it reused or recycled? Ask permission to take this packaging home and add it to your packaging per ounce calculations.

take action

There are lots of ways you can reduce the amount of packaging you and your family send to the landfill.

Buy big.
Join a buying club that sells most everything you need in large quantities with much less packaging. But pay attention—not everything available in bulk uses less packaging. For example, if you're buying spaghetti sauce, make sure you're getting an extra

large jar instead of three regular jars sold together in a box. If the quantities are too huge for your small family, go shopping with neighbors or friends and share the expense and the products. Don't forget to remind everyone to recycle.

Buy in bins.
Many products such as nuts, grains, dried fruits, pasta, granola, flour, and even candy, peanut butter, oils, and syrups are now sold by the pound. You can purchase just the amount you need with very little packaging. You can even bring your own bags and bottles.

Join a farm.

One way to get rid of packaging is to get your produce from a farm. And with Community Supported Agriculture (CSAs) you can do this even if you don't live anywhere near one. You can buy a membership to a farm, and you'll receive a basket of produce every week during growing season. The produce comes fresh and unpackaged and you even have to return the basket in order to get your next week's supply.

Pack your snack.
Once you've bought your bulk-sized snacks, pack your own individual servings into reusable bags or containers. All those individual-sized snacks really pack on the wrappings.

Look for a sign.

Look for the recycling symbol (three arrows in a sort of triangle). This indicates that the packaging is made from recycled material. Packaging can be made from *pre-consumer* (leftovers from the factory or damaged products that never made it to a store) or *post-consumer* (paper, plastic, and metal that you recycled) materials.

Don't use foam products.
Foam packing products (or *expanded polystyrene*) are not recyclable in most places, but they can be reused. Contact a local shipping store to see if they will reuse foam peanuts and other packing materials. Newer biodegradable packing materials made from cornstarch are now widely available.

Eat fruit instead of drinking juice.
Fruit comes in its own primary packaging. And if you buy it from a farmer's market, there's much less secondary and tertiary packaging. And no little sticker.

Think twice before buying fast food.
Even when you "eat in" all your food will be wrapped or contained in some sort of disposable product. And if you get it "to go," well that's at least one more bag that will end up in the landfill. And do you really need all those extra ketchup packets, napkins, and straws? Take just what you need, and

save any extra napkins in the glove box for next time. Try to eat in places that use washable plates and forks, and sit down to enjoy your meal.

Disappearing Waste

Maybe you've had this thought while cleaning your room: What if you could just make all the stuff you don't want and don't need disappear? Normally, this sort of "magic act" involves throwing stuff in the garbage. Then the garbage is carted off to the landfill and you never see it again (hopefully). But what if the garbage just disappeared? Scientists have been working on ways to make different things we use biodegradable. This means microbes in the soil break these items down, essentially making them disappear.

Note: You do not have the right microbes in your room to make this a time-efficient solution to your cleaning problems.

JUST THE FACTS

* 90% of solid waste goes into landfills.

* Waste from houses and apartments makes up about 60% of all solid waste. The rest comes from hospitals, schools, and businesses.

* About one-third of the trash in a landfill is packaging.

Clockwise from top: Cornstarch packing peanuts that dissolve in water; polystyrene containers that won't biodegrade any time soon; steam rising from compost; palm-frond baskets from China—100% biodegradable.

THE EXPERIMENT
How do environmental conditions affect how disposable grocery bags decompose?

Summary

You'll place plastic and paper bags in different environments to see how quickly the bags decompose. This experiment will take three or four months to complete, so start early!

What You Need

- 4 biodegradable plastic grocery bags
- 4 non biodegradable plastic grocery bags
- 4 paper shopping bags
- Sunny location in a yard
- Mallet
- 9 wooden stakes
- Shovel
- Pitchfork
- Use of a compost pile
- 3 containers, 3-gallon (11.4 l) capacity
- Water
- Rock (optional)
- Camera

Experimental Procedure

1. Secure one of each type of bag to the ground at the same sunny location in a yard. Use the mallet to pound two stakes through each bag. You don't want them to blow away in the middle of your experiment.

2. Dig three holes 1 foot (30.5 cm) deep with a shovel. Place one of each of the bags in each hole and fill in the holes with dirt. (You want each bag to be in the same type of soil, so bury them close to each other, but make sure there's at least 6 inches [15 cm] between each bag.) Use the remaining stakes to mark the locations of the holes.

3. Use the pitchfork to help you place one of each of the bags in the middle of the compost pile. Rake the removed compost material back over the bags. The bags should not be touching.

4. Fill each of the 3-gallon (11.4 l) containers to the brim with water.

5. Place the last three bags in the containers. Put a rock in each one to sink the bag if you want.

6. Leave the bags where they are for three to four months.

7. Dig up the buried bags and record how each bag changed in the different locations. Take a photo of each bag. You can use the photos on your display.

Conclusion

Be very descriptive in comparing the bags in each of the location. Describe what they looked like, including whether there were holes in the bags or pieces missing. Which bags do you think decomposed the most? The least? Did one type of bag decompose more than the rest at each location or were the results mixed?

Take a Closer Look

A product is biodegradable if it will break down safely and relatively quickly when exposed to naturally occurring microbes in water or soil. Microbes, usually bacteria, gobble up whatever they find in the soil. Some things are easier for them to eat than others. Biodegradable items take advantage of these microbes, so they're usually made from starches, vegetable oils, and other materials that are easy for bacteria to eat. Plastics made from petroleum are not as easy for these microbes to eat.

Manufacturers still can't agree on how safely and quickly something needs to decompose to be labeled "biodegradable." Calling something biodegradable can mean a lot of things. Most biodegradable products will break down within one to 10 years. More importantly, biodegradable products should not produce harmful chemicals as they break down. For example, some detergents biodegrade into carbolic acid, which is toxic to fish. These detergents shouldn't be labeled "biodegradable."

Test Your Brain

How long does it take these common items to decompose?

A. Wool socks	1. 1–12 years
B. Plastic six-pack holders	2. 5 years
C. Leather shoes	3. 450 years
D. Glass bottles	4. 10–20 years
E. Cigarette butts	5. 1–5 years
F. Aluminum cans	6. Forever
G. Milk cartons	7. 80–100 years
H. Paper	8. 6 months
I. Plastic bags	9. 1 million years
J. Orange peels	10. 2–5 months
K. Plastic bottles	11. 25–40 years

Answers: A-5, B-3, C-11, D-9, E-1, F-7, G-2, H-10, I-4, J-8, K-6

take action

Start Composting

Don't put all those biodegradable products in the landfill—start a compost pile.

You'll need three things to make a good compost pile: water, air, and stuff to compost. (Good things to compost include dried leaves, sticks, grass clippings, and food waste from your kitchen.)

To make a simple, no hassle compost pile without fancy equipment, follow these instructions:

Find a place that
- you can dig a hole (ask permission!)
- gets morning light
- is shaded in the afternoon
- is near a hose or other water source

For a good-sized compost pile you'll need to dig a hole about 12 inches (30.5 cm) deep and at least 4 feet (1.2 m) across. The hole helps stop the pile from spreading, keeps air and moisture in, and allows earthworms and beneficial microbes to migrate into your pile.

Lay a bunch of twigs and small sticks (no bigger around than your fingers) on the bottom of your hole. These will help create air pockets in your compost pile. Add a few more inches of dry material such as leaves and twigs. Shredded newspaper and paper egg cartons are good, too. You might even want to buy a bag of manure at the garden store to jump-start the microbes.

Finally, add a few inches of green material such as fresh grass clippings. Add kitchen refuse such as tea bags, eggshells, vegetable peelings, and plate scrapings that don't include meat or fat. Never add meat and oils (they attract animals and don't break down quickly) and dog and cat poop (because of disease).

Water the pile so that it's good and wet but there are no puddles. The microbes that eat up all this yummy compost like to stay damp. Top off your pile with a few shovelfuls of the dirt you dug out of the hole. This will provide all the microbes that are going to dig into the compost feast.

Continue adding layers to your pile by alternating brown (dry) material with green (fresh) material. Don't forget to throw in all the biodegradable trash, too. You don't have to be too picky about the layers.

After about six months you should be ready to add the compost to your garden. You know it's ready when you can't tell a leaf from a banana peel and the pile looks kind of dark, loose, and fluffy. Your garden will be really happy.

rethinking POLLUTION

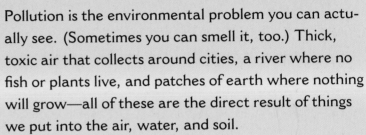

Pollution is the environmental problem you can actually see. (Sometimes you can smell it, too.) Thick, toxic air that collects around cities, a river where no fish or plants live, and patches of earth where nothing will grow—all of these are the direct result of things we put into the air, water, and soil.

Air pollution's primary source is burning fossil fuels and car emissions. The chemicals released into the air cause problems both high in the atmosphere (carbon dioxide and methane creating the greenhouse effect) and down near the surface where we live. People breathe in pollutants such as ozone and dust, which damage their lungs. Worldwide, many people suffer from respiratory illnesses and asthma caused by air pollution.

Putting chemicals directly into lakes, rivers, or the oceans can cause water pollution. But the biggest causes of water pollution are from the chemicals we spray, pour, and dump on the ground. Rain and groundwater carry these pollutants into streams, ponds, rivers, lakes, and oceans. This can kill the plants and animals that live in the water, and it makes it harder to find clean drinking water. Scientists have recently discovered that lots of the medicines people take are also ending up in our water supply. We don't yet know what effect (if any) that will have on our health.

Of all the threats to the Earth, pollution has been studied the most because it doesn't hide—we can see, smell, and taste it. But our desire for greener lawns, bigger cars, and fancy electronic gadgets that require lots of electricity means more pollutants not fewer. So we're going to have to find other ways to keep the Earth healthy without burning fossil fuels and dumping chemicals in our water.

The projects in this chapter explore air pollution from ozone and carbon dioxide, alternatives to common household chemicals that pollute, and light pollution.

Heating Up

You've probably heard all sorts of things about carbon dioxide. This little molecule has been accused of heating up the Earth, causing hurricanes, changing weather patterns, and even making life more difficult for polar bears. But did you know that life wouldn't exist on Earth without carbon dioxide? It's an essential part of our atmosphere. That doesn't mean we're not in trouble. The greenhouse effect (see page 69) describes what is happening to Earth because there is now too much carbon dioxide in the air. How did it get there? You guessed it: our over reliance on fossil fuels. So, just how does the extra carbon dioxide make the planet warm up?

JUST THE FACTS

* Without any greenhouse gases in the atmosphere, the Earth's surface would be 60°F (33°C) colder.

* In the past 25 years, more than 20% of the polar ice cap has melted.

* The number of tropical storms and hurricanes in the Atlantic Ocean has increased by 40% in the last 10 years from about nine storms per year to about 14 storms per year. Global warming may be causing this increase.

* 75% of the carbon dioxide released into the air is from burning fossil fuels.

* The average car produces 5 tons (4,500 kg) of carbon dioxide each year.

THE EXPERIMENT

How does the amount of carbon dioxide in the air affect how much the air heats up when exposed to sunlight?

Summary

You'll fill bottles with different amounts of carbon dioxide (CO_2) gas and measure the change in temperature inside the bottles as they sit in the Sun.

What You Need

- Five 20-ounce (590 ml) soda bottles, clean and empty
- Funnel
- Measuring spoons
- Baking soda
- 5 thermometers*
- White vinegar
- Stopwatch
- Bright sunlight

*The thermometers need to fit inside the bottles.

Experimental Procedure

1. Clean and dry the soda bottles.

2. Use the funnel to carefully pour 2 teaspoons (10 ml) of baking soda in one bottle, 4 teaspoons (20 ml) in another, and 8 teaspoons (40 ml) in the last bottle. The other two bottles won't have anything in them. Label each bottle with the amount of baking soda it contains.

3. Drop a thermometer into each of the bottles, including the empty ones. Make sure they're down far enough that you can tightly screw the cap back on the bottles.

4. Working quickly, pour vinegar into the bottle with 8 teaspoons (39.4 ml) of baking soda. Pour in enough vinegar to more than cover the baking soda. Immediately screw the cap on as tight as you can. Shake the bottle gently so that all of the baking soda reacts with the vinegar.

5. Repeat step 4 for the other bottles containing baking soda.

6. Let all the bottles sit indoors (out of the Sun) for 20 minutes so that the vinegar and baking soda finish reacting and the remaining gas and liquid warm back up to room temperature.

7. While you're waiting, screw the cap tightly onto one of the empty bottles and make sure the other cap is removed. You'll compare the temperatures in the baking soda/vinegar bottles to these bottles.

8. Once all the bottles are at room temperature, record the starting temperature and take them outside to a warm, sunny spot. Make sure they aren't touching each other and are each receiving direct sunlight. Leave them in the Sun for 20 minutes.

9. After 20 minutes, record the temperature in each bottle.

An oil refinery tower burning natural gas

Conclusion

When you added vinegar to the baking soda, the reaction produces carbon dioxide gas (CO_2). (That was all the fizzy bubbling you saw in the bottles.) Although we don't know exactly how much CO_2 is in each bottle, we do know the relative amounts. The bottle with 4 teaspoons (19.7 ml) of baking soda has twice as much CO_2 as the bottle with 2 teaspoons (9.9 ml). The bottle with 8 teaspoons (39.4 ml) of baking soda has twice as much CO_2 as the bottle with 4 teaspoons (19.7 ml).

Subtract the starting temperature from the final temperature to get the change in temperature for each bottle. Create a line graph of the amount of baking soda versus the change in temperature in the sunlight. How is the change in temperature in sunlight related to the amount of carbon dioxide in the bottles? How did the temperature change of the two control bottles compare to the temperature change in the bottles with CO_2?

Take a Closer Look

Carbon dioxide is a *greenhouse gas*. It absorbs heat that radiated off the Earth and sends it right back down to the Earth. Carbon dioxide itself is colorless and odorless—you usually don't even know it's there. Trees and plants recycle carbon dioxide when they photosynthesize, converting carbon dioxide, light energy, and water into oxygen and food for the plant.

Excessive greenhouse gases are caused by the carbon dioxide released by burning fossil fuels. Cutting down large areas of forests adds to the problem because the dead plants can't soak up carbon dioxide and turn it into oxygen. Because we depend so much on fossil fuels for transportation, electricity, heating, and cooling, it doesn't appear as if things are going to cool down anytime soon unless we make some big changes.

*Explore*Further

Try this experiment on a cool sunny day and a hot sunny day, in the evening and in the morning. Do your results vary with air temperature or time of day? Can you test other greenhouse gases such as water vapor or methane?

A good view spoiled by smog

take action

You don't have to live in a tent to help reduce greenhouse gases. The ideas listed below will keep more than 10 tons (9,000 kg) of carbon dioxide out of the atmosphere each year.

Change your light bulbs.

As your regular light bulbs burn out, replace them with compact fluorescents (CFLs). The switch will keep about 300 pounds (130 kg) of CO_2 from entering the atmosphere a year.

Monitor the thermostat.

In the winter, keep the thermostat 2° lower than usual and up 2° in summer. Almost half of the energy we use in our homes goes to heating and cooling. You could save about 2,000 pounds (900 kg) of CO_2 a year by wearing a sweater in the winter and cool clothing in the summer months.

Take shorter, cooler showers.

It takes a lot of energy to heat water. You can use less hot water by installing a low-flow showerhead (to keep 350 pounds [160 kg] of CO_2 out of our air per year) and washing your clothes in cold or warm water instead of hot (to save 500 pounds [230 kg] per year).

Dry your clothes on a clothesline.

You can keep 700 pounds [300 kg] of CO_2 from our atmosphere when you air dry your clothes for six months out of the year.

Recycle (of course).

You can save 2,400 pounds (1,000 kg) of CO_2 a year by recycling half of the garbage you throw out.

Turn off your TV.

Simply turning off your television, DVD player, stereo, and computer when you're not using them will save up to 3,000 pounds (1,300 kg] of CO_2 a year.

Unplug your appliances.

Even when turned off, things like hair dryers, cell phone chargers, and televisions use energy. In fact, the energy used to keep display clocks lit and memory chips working sends 18 million tons (16 billion kg) of CO_2 into the atmosphere every year.

Plant a tree (or several).

A single tree will absorb 1 ton (900 kg) of CO_2 over its lifetime.

Buy local, fresh and organic.

The average meal travels 1,200 miles (2,000 km) to get to your mouth. That generates almost 1,000 pounds (450 kg) of CO_2 for each meal! Eating local and fresh food will keep that carbon dioxide out of the atmosphere. Organic soils soak up extra CO_2 from the air a lot faster than regular farm soil, so buying organic helps too.

Ride the bus, your bike, or walk.

Reducing the amount you are driven by 10 miles (16 km) every week can eliminate about 500 pounds (230 kg) of CO_2 emissions a year.

How The Greenhouse Effect Works

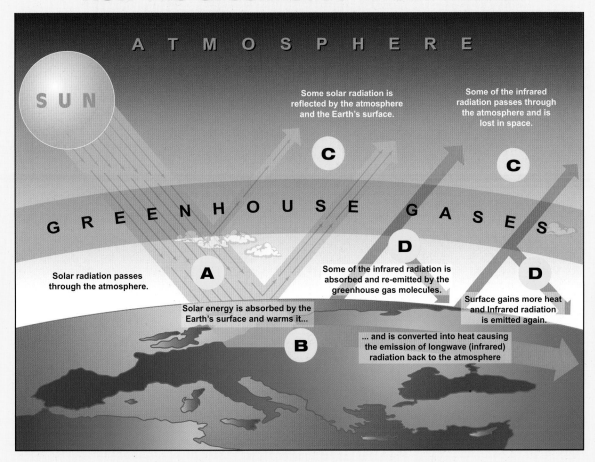

You've heard of the greenhouse effect, but do you actually know how it works?

Basically, our atmosphere is a blanket that lets some of the Sun's energy in but not out so that the Earth is just the right temperature. The Sun sends us energy through its light rays **(A)**. A lot of that energy is visible light but some of it is ultraviolet and infrared light. The visible and infrared light warm up the land and water **(B)**.

The land and oceans soak up about 70% of the visible light from the Sun. As they heat up, they give off heat in the form of infrared light or heat **(C)**. The greenhouse effect happens when our atmosphere gets in the way **(D)**.

The atmosphere is mostly made of nitrogen, oxygen, and argon—gases that don't interact a whole lot with the infrared light. However, there is also water vapor, carbon dioxide, and methane (the greenhouse gases) in the atmosphere that soak up and trap some of the infrared radiation instead of letting it go out into space.

Now, a little bit of this trapping is good. It keeps us from entering another ice age. But lately, we've been burning fossil fuels and pumping more carbon dioxide and methane up into the atmosphere than needed. This means that we are trapping more heat here on Earth, causing our polar ice to melt, the oceans to warm, weather to get wilder, and all the other effects of a warmer planet.

If that wasn't bad enough, the warmer we get, the harder it is to turn things around. That's because water vapor, which is also a greenhouse gas, traps four times as much heat as carbon dioxide! And the warmer it gets, the more water evaporates into the air, which makes it even warmer.

Since we can't exactly get rid of water in the air—we need it to live and clouds give us shade and rain—we need to focus on keeping the other greenhouse gases from getting into the air.

No-zone

During the summer, you may hear a lot about ozone alerts. These are times when there's too much ozone in the air, making it potentially hazardous to your health. In fact, on certain days people may be encouraged not to go outside if at all possible because there's so much ozone. Just what is this ozone, and are there places where it's more concentrated?

JUST THE FACTS

* There are only three ozone molecules for every 10 million air molecules.

* 90% of the ozone is in the stratosphere (10 to 30 miles [10 to 50 km] above the Earth). This is known as the *ozone layer* and it protects the Earth from ultraviolet (UV) radiation from the Sun.

* 10% of the ozone is near the Earth's surface where it's toxic.

* In the United States, pollution from ozone near the ground kills $500 million worth of crops per year.

THE EXPERIMENT

How does distance from a road affect the
amount of ozone measured in the air?

Adult
Supervision
Required

Summary

You'll make ozone test papers and then place them at
different distances from a busy road.

What You Need

- Measuring cup
- Distilled water
- Glass bowl or pot*
  Measuring spoons
- Cornstarch
- Plastic spoon
- Stovetop or hot plate and adult supervision
- Hot pad or mitt
- Potassium Iodide (KI)**
- Coffee filters
- Glass or ceramic plate
- Small paintbrush
- Paper
- Scissors
- Sealable plastic bag
- Measuring tape
- Spray bottle
- Map of the area where you'll test the ozone

* You can order this from a chemical supply company or your
teacher may have some.

** This pot will be used on the stovetop. Don't use a metal pot—the
metal will react with the chemicals.

Experimental Procedure

1. First, you have to make the ozone test papers.
   Place 4 cups (0.9 l) of distilled water in the
   glass bowl or pot. Add 1 1/4 teaspoon (6.2 ml)
   of cornstarch. Heat and stir with the plastic
   spoon until the mixture thickens and becomes
   somewhat see-through.

2. Remove the pot from the stove and add 1/4
   teaspoon (1.2 ml) of Potassium Iodide (KI). Stir
   the mixture. Let the paste cool in the pot.

3. Cut the coffee filters open so the filters are only
   one layer. Lay one filter on a glass or ceramic
   plate. Carefully brush the paste onto both sides
   of the filter using the small paintbrush. Apply
   the paste as uniformly as possible.

4. Make as many test papers as you have paste.
   It's better to have too many than too few.

5. Lay the wet test papers on a piece of plain
   paper in a dark, dry place to dry out.

6. When the test papers are dry, cut them into
   1-inch-wide (2.5 cm) strips. Wash your hands
   well. Potassium Iodide isn't toxic but it can
   cause mild skin irritation.

7. To store the test papers, place them in a sealed
   plastic bag and keep them in a dark place.

8. Now you're ready to test the ozone. Find a
   busy road that you can get to easily, such as the
   one in front of your school. Check with an adult
   to make sure this is a safe area. They might
   want to come with you.

9. Find a spot as close to the road as you can get
   where your test paper won't be disturbed, is
   out of direct sunlight, and can be left for about
   eight hours. Locate at least three other spots at
   various distances from the road and, if possible,
   away from other car traffic. Also, find one spot
   indoors that you can use as a control.

10. Use a measuring tape to measure how far away
    each test paper is from the road. Write this
    number in your lab book.

11. Spray each test paper with distilled water and
    hang each one at a chosen data collection site.
    It's very important that the paper be out of
    direct sunlight and can hang freely. You'll also
    get better results if it isn't very humid.

12. Let the test papers hang for about eight hours.

13. Collect the test papers and seal them in
    separate plastic bags.

High
Ozone

Low
Ozone

No
Ozone

14. To see the results, spray the test papers one at a time with distilled water. Compare the color of your strip to the guide on the left. Record the color of each strip in your lab notebook.

Conclusion

Make a bar graph of distance (on the x-axis) versus ozone level (none, low, medium, or high)? Is there a pattern? Where was the ozone highest and where was it lowest?

Take a Closer Look

The ozone test papers you made use a chemical reaction to detect the ozone in the air. Ozone reacts with the potassium iodide and water to produce oxygen, iodine, and potassium hydroxide. Then the iodine reacts with the cornstarch and turns purple.

Ozone is made up of three oxygen atoms joined together (O_3), which makes it very different from the oxygen we breathe, which is two oxygen atoms joined together (O_2).

Up high in the air of the *stratosphere* (up to 30 miles [50 km] above the Earth) ozone protects Earth from the Sun's harmful UV rays, which

*Explore*Further

What other factors do you think affect ozone levels? How about time of day, temperature, humidity, time of year, or even other pollutants in the air?

Go online and locate ozone data for you area. Compare your results to those reported by local weather services.

Based on your experiment and research, see if you can predict the ozone levels in other locations. Test your predictions.

cause sunburn and skin cancer. The ozone in the stratosphere bounces the rays back into space, protecting us from the harmful radiation.

But the ozone down near Earth's surface (called the *troposphere*) where we breathe is not so good. Ground-level ozone is an air pollutant found in smog. It's bad for people and animals to breathe, and it also damages crops, trees, and plants. Ozone is formed in the troposphere when chemicals given off by car exhaust, gasoline vapors, factories, and other polluters react with the energy in sunlight.

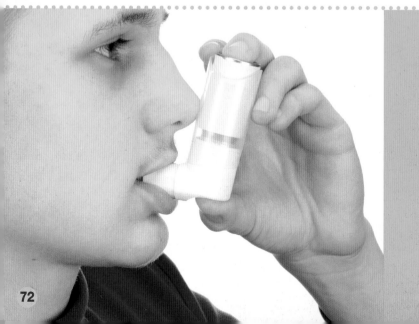

Why is Ozone Bad?

Ozone is a powerful cleaner, disinfectant, and bleaching agent. This is what also makes ozone dangerous. When it comes in contact with our lungs, ozone attacks and damages cells lining the airways. This can cause swelling and inflammation.

Ozone in our air can also cause sore throats, coughing, reduced lung function, asthma attacks, emphysema, bronchitis, and may reduce the body's ability to fight infections in the respiratory system.

Lights Out!

Y̲ou wouldn't think of leaving your home without turning off the lights, would you? Well, there are buildings, parking lots, malls, and even whole cities that leave the lights on even when nobody's "home." All these lights left on create light pollution. This not only wastes energy, but also creates problems for stargazers, nocturnal animals, night-blooming flowers, and maybe even your own health. Don't think light pollution is much of a problem? Try counting the stars tonight.

JUST THE FACTS

* Between 4 and 40 million birds are killed each year from being attracted to (and flying into) tall, brightly lit buildings.

* On average, sky glow makes it impossible for 21% of people on Earth to even see one of the brightest sky features—the Milky Way.

* Urban sky glow is increasing by about 30% each year in large cities in the United States.

* 35% to 50% of light pollution is caused by roadway lighting.

* Low-pressure sodium roadway lights are 10 times more efficient than incandescent lights and produce less light pollution.

* Someone standing on the north rim of the Grand Canyon can see the sky glow from Las Vegas, over 175 miles (282 km) away.

THE EXPERIMENT
How does location affect light pollution?

Summary

You'll count the visible stars in different areas to measure the light pollution in your community.

What You Need

- Adult who will stay up late with you
- Ruler
- Scissors
- Heavy paper or card stock
- String
- Masking tape
- Red cellophane
- Flashlight
- Night with a new Moon

Safety Warning – Don't wander around outdoors in the dark without an adult.

Experimental Procedure

1. First, make a frame to use when counting the stars. (This will help make sure the area in which you're counting stars stays the same.) Cut an 8-inch (20.3 cm) square out of the piece of paper. Measure 1 inch (2.5 cm) in from the edge of your square all the way around. Cut out the middle so that you have a 7-inch (17.8 cm) square hole in the middle of the frame.

2. Use the scissors to cut a piece of string 16 inches (40.6 cm) long. Tape one end to the corner of your frame. When you're ready to start your experiment, you'll tape the other end to your shoulder. The string will help you hold the frame the same distance from your body each time you use it. When you look through the frame at the stars, you'll see about $1/40^{th}$ of the sky.

3. Tape red cellophane over the top of the flashlight. You'll need to use the flashlight to write down your data when you're counting stars. Your eyes will be able to adjust more quickly to the dark if you use a red light.

4. Choose at least six locations with different lighting conditions to measure the light pollution. For example, you could count stars under a streetlight, in the middle of your backyard, and at the neighborhood park. Or, if you can get your adult helper to drive you, try to use a couple of locations out in the country and a couple near a city or town. Just be sure that a good chunk of the sky is clear from trees, buildings, and other stuff that will block your view. Take your measurements on a clear night with a new Moon (or when the Moon is not up yet) at least one hour after the Sun has set.

5. At your first location, look through the frame at the stars. Hold the frame steady and carefully, and count how many stars you see inside it. Write down your location and the number of stars. It helps if you're familiar with a few constellations so you know your locations. Wait a few minutes after you turn out the flashlight for your eyes to adjust before counting stars.

6. Repeat step 5 four more times, looking at different pieces of the sky. You should have a total of five star counts for each location.

7. Repeat steps 5 and 6 for each of your locations.

Conclusion

Average the five star counts for each location. Since the frame allows you to see about $1/40^{th}$ of the sky, multiply the average number of stars in the frame by 40. This is the approximate number of stars you could see in the sky at that location. Make a bar graph of location versus the number of visible stars.

What location showed you the most stars? What location showed you the least? The number of stars you could see is directly related to the light pollution in that location. Which areas had the most light pollution? A perfectly clear, dark sky will let you see about 1,500 stars. Were you able to see anything close to this?

Take a Closer Look

Light can pollute in many different ways, depending on what causes the light and where it shines. If your neighbor's porch light shines into your bedroom window, this is called *light trespass*. Really bright lights that actually make it harder to see can cause *glare*. The biggest problem is often *sky glow*, when all the lights from a city or even just a sports arena reflect off buildings, the ground, and clouds to make the sky much brighter than it should be.

Light pollution is a waste of energy, but what other effects does it have?

Too much light can cause sleep deprivation, headaches, high blood pressure, and stress. Not enough dark time at night can also make your body produce less *melatonin*, which helps your immune system and lets your body know when it's time to sleep.

Extra light at night, can be really bad for animals and ecosystems. Flowers that are pollinated by moths can die off. The moths are far more attracted to the bright lights than the flowers that give them food. The flowers don't get pollinated, and the moths starve. Also, certain types of algae and plants keep growing when light is shining on them. In ponds, these plants suck up all the oxygen in the water, so fish and frogs can't survive there.

Nocturnal animals have the opposite problem. If it's too bright at night, they can starve because they're blinded by the light and can't hunt for food. These animals also have trouble waking up, because it doesn't ever seem to get dark.

Baby sea turtles are also in danger from light pollution. They use the light of the Moon reflected on the water to find their way from the sand to the ocean. Because of light pollution, many are fooled into following streetlights, crawling out onto parking lots and roads.

Explore Further

Compare the number of stars you can see from the backyard when all the lights in your house are on to the number of stars you can see when all the lights are turned off. See if you can get all of your neighbors to turn off their lights for this experiment. Invite everyone outside for a star counting party!

take action

With private space flight just around the corner, it won't be long before there could be billboards in space orbiting Earth. Then we could see light pollution coming from the sky down to Earth rather than the other way around. In 1993, the US Congress passed a law prohibiting all "obtrusive advertising" in space. What are some things that you can do in your home or neighborhood to reduce light pollution, besides passing a law against it?

- Turn off the lights when you're not using them.

- Add light and motion sensors to outside lights. This way they'll only come on when they're needed.

- Add shields to outdoor lights so that the light only goes down instead of in all directions.

- Celebrate National Dark Sky Week, held on the week of the new Moon in April. Talk to your friends and neighbors about the effects of light pollution and easy ways we can prevent it.

- Ask billboard companies to stop lighting billboards at night, or to adjust the lights so they shine down instead of up.

- Talk to your local government about using sodium lamps in streetlights instead of fluorescent or incandescent light bulbs. Sodium lamps use less energy and produce less sky glow.

Bright Lights, Big Cities

Imagine it was nighttime all over the globe at the same time. The photo below represents the light pollution you could see from space. (This photograph is actually a composite of hundreds of photos taken from NASA satellites.) How many countries and major cities can you locate simply by the amount of light pollution they emit? Get a map of the world and see how many you picked. Or, go to http://www-static.cc.gatech.edu/~pesti/night/r to see a map superimposed over this image.

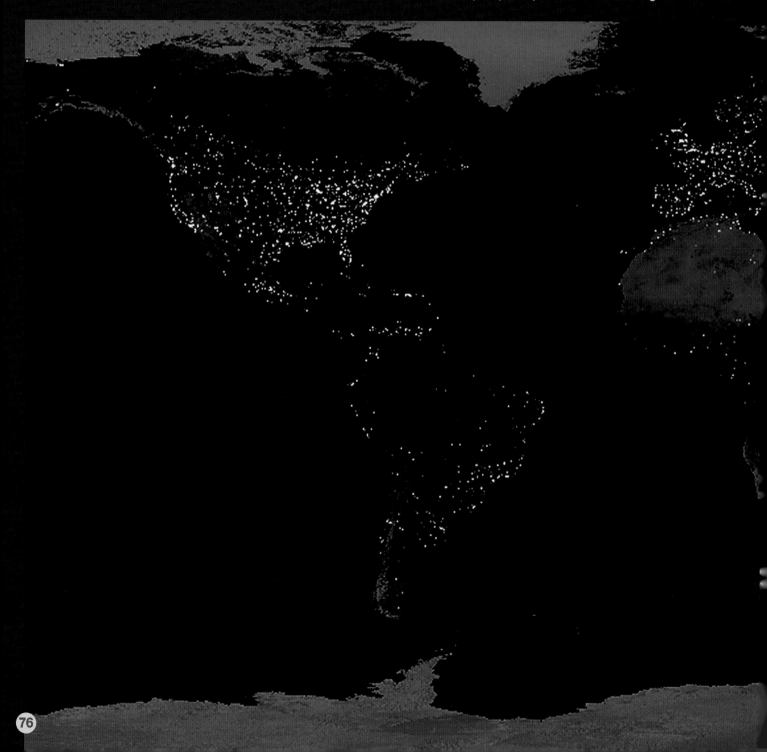

This photo and ones like it give scientists lots of information on just how urbanized the world is becoming. For one thing, pinpricks of light are now appearing in unlikely places, such as the Amazon jungle and Siberia. Also, since urban development changes the landscape, soil, climate, and ecosytem, scientists map this development so they can predict weather changes, population, possible food shortages, and other environmental impacts.

Clean Up Your Act

Take a look under the kitchen sink and wherever else cleaners are stored in your home. How many different cleaners can you find? Look at the labels. How many of them say things like "poisonous," "dangerous," or "toxic"? If the chemicals in the cleaners will make *you* sick, what do you think they'll do to the rest of the planet? This experiment tests how non-toxic cleaners stack up next to toxic ones.

JUST THE FACTS

* The average home uses 10 gallons (40 l) of harmful chemicals each year.

* Indoor air pollution is about 100 times higher than outdoor air pollution.

* In an average year in the United States, more than 20,000 children under age 6 are exposed to poisonous levels of chlorine bleach.

* More than 275 active ingredients in antibacterial soaps and cleaners are classified as pesticides.

* 76% of all liquid soaps and 29% of bar soaps now contain anti-bacterial chemicals.

Summary

You'll grow bacteria in Petri dishes with different types of disinfecting cleaners. You'll measure the area on the dish where the cleaners stopped the growth of bacteria.

What You Need

- Agar*
- 30 sterile Petri dishes**
- Refrigerator
- Hole punch
- Blotter paper or a thick paper towel
- Tablespoon
- White vinegar
- Hydrogen peroxide
- Lemon juice
- Water
- Commercial disinfecting cleaner (whatever you have around the house)
- 6 glasses
- Baking soda
- Spoon
- Permanent marker and masking tape
- Test tube
- Filtered water
- 30 cotton swabs
- Tweezers
- Cardboard box
- Ruler
- Latex gloves
- Bleach
- Garbage bag

* You can get this from a science supply company, either on its own or already in a Petri dish.

** Available from science supply companies.

Experimental Procedure

1. If your agar isn't already in the Petri dishes, carefully read the directions, prepare the agar, and pour it into the sterile Petri dishes. Make sure the agar is set and cooled before inoculating it in step 7. Always store the Petri dishes upside down (with the agar at the top of the dish) in a fridge until you're ready to use them. This will keep water from condensing on the agar.

2. Use the hole-punch on the blotter paper or paper towel to make 30 dots.

3. Pour 5 tablespoons (73.9 ml) of each liquid cleaner (vinegar, hydrogen peroxide, lemon juice, water, and commercial cleaner) into five different glasses.

4. In the last glass, pour 4 tablespoons (59.1 ml) of water and 2 tablespoons (29.6 ml) of baking soda. Mix the solution until the baking soda is completely dissolved in the water.

5. Place five paper dots in each cup. You might need to poke them down with a spoon so they're completely covered by the liquid. Let the dots sit in the cups for one hour so that they soak up the cleaners.

6. Use the permanent marker and masking tape to label the bottom of the Petri dishes with a type of cleaner. You'll have five dishes for each type of cleaner.

7. Fill the test tube with a small amount of filtered water. Rub a cotton swab along the floor for a few seconds. Now the swab is coated with bacteria. Dip it into the water in the test tube to transfer some of the bacteria you collected into the water. Now, inoculate a Petri dish by pouring the water into the dish so the entire surface of the agar is covered. Pour out any extra water.

8. Repeat step 7 for all of the Petri dishes. Be sure to use fresh water, a clean cotton swab, and a different piece of floor each time. Wash out the test tube each time.

9. Use tweezers to carefully remove the dots from the cup containing vinegar. Place one dot in the center of the agar in each Petri dish labeled "vinegar." Rinse off the tweezers and then do the same for each of the other cleaners. Cover the dishes after you're done.

10. Use the masking tape to seal the edges of the dishes, but be sure that you can still see the top surface of the agar clearly. DO NOT OPEN THE PETRI DISHES after this step until you're ready to throw them away. The bacteria growing on the agar could make you sick.

11. Place all the dishes upside down in a box. The dots should stick to the agar. Put the box in a warm, dry place. Above the refrigerator is a good spot.

12. Each day bring down the box of Petri dishes and observe what has happened. Write down any changes you notice. You can even take photos or sketch pictures of the Petri dishes.

13. After seven days, you should notice that bacteria colonies are growing just about

everywhere, except around the dot you soaked in cleaner. There will be a circle around the dots that is free of bacteria. Use your ruler to measure the diameter (how far across) of each circle. Bigger circles mean the cleaner is a better disinfectant.

14. To dispose of the Petri dishes, put on latex gloves. Hold each dish over the sink and pour a small amount of bleach over the bacteria colonies growing on the agar. Don't get any bleach on your skin, eyes, or clothes. It will burn. **Don't do this if the cleaners you're testing contain ammonia.** (If you're not sure, don't do it—just throw the dishes away.) Then, re-close all of the dishes and seal them in a garbage bag before throwing them away.

Conclusion

Average the diameters of the circles for each type of cleaner. These circles are called *kill zones* because that is where the bacteria are killed. Make a bar graph of cleaner type versus kill zone size. Which cleaner had the largest kill zone and was most effective at preventing the bacteria from growing? What other observations did you make?

Compare the hazard and safety warnings on the containers for all of the cleaners you used. How does the safety of the cleaners compare to its ability to kill bacteria?

Take a Closer Look

A toxic cleaner will make you sick if it is inhaled, swallowed, or makes contact with your skin. Non-toxic cleaners won't—at least not in small doses. (Anything can make you sick if you eat or drink too much of it.) In fact, most non-toxic cleaners such as vinegar, lemon juice, and baking soda are used in cooking. Hydrogen peroxide is used to disinfect cuts and scrapes on your skin.

Many commercial cleaners contain dangerous chemicals. Even when they're locked up tight and out of reach, they can release toxic or *irritating volatile organic compounds (VOCs)* into the air. For example,

paradichlorobenzenes used in toilet fresheners and room deodorizers, and formaldehyde used in disinfectants and furniture polishes, might cause cancer. Aerosol spray disinfectants and solvent-based spot removers contain other VOCs that pollute the air and cause smog.

And it isn't just your health that's in danger. Toxic cleaners can wreak havoc on the environment, too. Phosphates, used in most dishwasher detergents, affect rivers and streams, causing algae to grow out of control. Too much algae keeps fish from getting the oxygen they need to live. Other cleaning chemicals don't biodegrade when you wash them down the drain. This can cause problems for plants and animals that drink the water when it finally gets back to the rivers and lakes. Manufacturing these cleaners creates environmental problems, as well.

*Explore*Further

Try other cleaners and collect your bacteria from different surfaces. Are some cleaners better in the bathroom and others better in the kitchen?

Some schools and medical offices use ultraviolet lights to disinfect goggles and medical equipment. See if you can get access to such a light box to observe whether or not ultraviolet light is effective at keeping bacteria from growing in the Petri dish.

The data you collected in this experiment is quantitative—you compared numbers from measurements. Collect some qualitative data, too. Ask your friends and family to try cleaning with vinegar and baking soda for a couple of weeks. Survey them afterward to find out how well they think these cleaners work compared to commercial cleaners.

Toxic cleaners are designed to kill germs—and the more germs they kill, the better. But we don't actually need to kill all the germs around us. Most of the microbes, such as bacteria and mold, are harmless. Bacteria naturally inhabit our skin, digestive tract, the soil, and our homes. In fact, there is even evidence that exposure to these germs is a good thing. They help make your immune system stronger so that you're less likely to develop allergies and asthma when you get older. All of these antibacterial cleaners are just overkill. Most of the time, soap and water are all you need to get rid of germs.

take action

Here are some recipes for non-toxic cleaners you can use at home.
Share them with your friends.

Window and mirror cleaner

Fill a spray bottle with ¼ cup (60 ml) of white vinegar then fill to the top with water. Shake the bottle to mix before spraying. Rub the window with a lint-free rag or a piece of wadded up newspaper.

Tub and sink cleaner

Sprinkle baking soda on the tub and sink and rub with a wet rag. Add a little liquid castile soap (vegetable oil soap) to the rag for more cleaning power.

Linoleum floor cleaner

Mop with a mixture of ½ cup (100 ml) vinegar in a pail of warm water.

Toilet bowl cleaner

Sprinkle baking soda inside the bowl. Add a couple drops of soap. Then scrub it with a toilet bowl brush.

Oven cleaner

Mix 1 cup (240 ml) of baking soda with enough water to make a paste. Apply to oven surfaces and let stand for about 15 minutes. Use a scouring pad for scrubbing. This recipe will require more scrubbing effort, but it isn't toxic. Don't use this recipe on self-cleaning ovens.

Deodorizer

Place an open box of baking soda in the fridge. Sprinkle it on carpets before vacuuming. Line the litter box with about 1 cup (240 ml) of baking soda before adding litter.

Drain cleaner

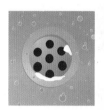

This recipe will free minor clogs and help to prevent future ones. Pour ½ cup (100 ml) of baking soda down the drain. Then pour in ½ cup (100 ml) of vinegar. Let it fizz for a few minutes. Then pour down several cups of boiling water. Repeat if needed.

Tarnish remover

Rub sliced lemons on brass, copper, bronze, and aluminum. This work especially well with baking soda sprinkled on the lemon.

Laundry brightener

Add ½ cup (100 ml) of strained lemon juice to the rinse cycle

Fabric rinse

Add ¼ cup (60 ml) of vinegar to the washing machine's rinse cycle to remove detergent completely from clothes, eliminating that scratchy feel. Do this instead of adding toxic fabric softener..

All-purpose cleaner

For spots on woodwork, tile, and linoleum, add a few drops of liquid soap to a wet washcloth and rub. Rinse and wipe thoroughly to remove any streaks.

If you want to get rid of leftover toxic cleaners, don't put them in the trash. They'll be toxic in a landfill, too. Contact your local landfill to find out when and where the next household hazardous waste collection will take place.

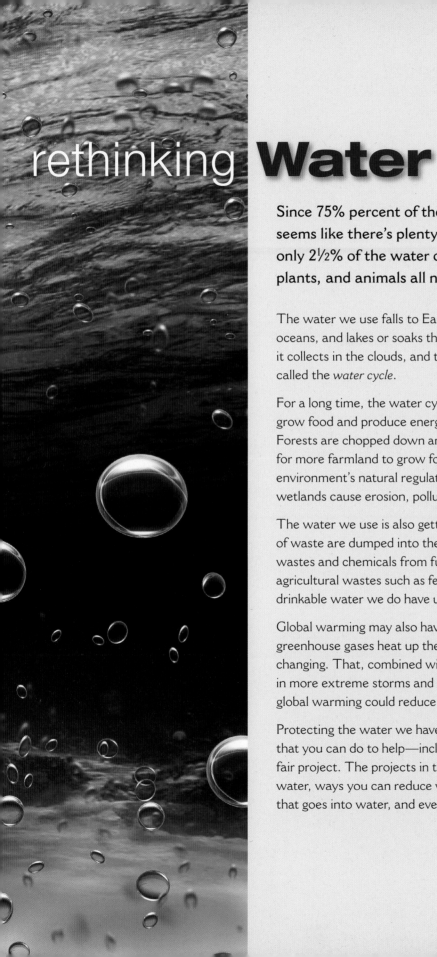

rethinking **Water**

Since 75% percent of the Earth is covered with water, it seems like there's plenty to go around, right? Unfortunately, only 2½% of the water on Earth is drinkable, and people, plants, and animals all need that water to live.

The water we use falls to Earth as rain and snow. It collects in rivers, oceans, and lakes or soaks through the ground. As the water evaporates, it collects in the clouds, and the process starts all over again. This is called the *water cycle*.

For a long time, the water cycle was pretty stable. But the way we grow food and produce energy has had an enormous impact on it. Forests are chopped down and wetlands are drained to make room for more farmland to grow food and graze animals. This disrupts the environment's natural regulation of water. More deforestation and fewer wetlands cause erosion, pollution, floods, and mudslides.

The water we use is also getting polluted. Worldwide, 2 million tons of waste are dumped into the water every day. This includes industrial wastes and chemicals from fuel production, human waste, and agricultural wastes such as fertilizers and pesticides. Pollution makes the drinkable water we do have undrinkable.

Global warming may also have enormous effects on the water cycle. As greenhouse gases heat up the Earth, the Earth's weather patterns are changing. That, combined with the melting Arctic and sea ice, will result in more extreme storms and higher sea levels. Scientists predict that global warming could reduce the amount of water we can use by 20%.

Protecting the water we have is really important. There are simple things that you can do to help—including exploring water use for your science fair project. The projects in this chapter look at how pollutants get into water, ways you can reduce water usage and the amount of pollution that goes into water, and even how to turn salt water into fresh water.

Down the Drain

People use water every day for drinking, cleaning, farming, and manufacturing. What would you do if there was no more water? Millions of people deal with this problem every day. Water shortages cause poverty and disease. Because of pollution, global warming, and irresponsible water use, water shortages could soon spread around the globe. Changing how you use water today can help solve the water crisis.

JUST THE FACTS

* More than 60% of your body is water.

* The world per-person, per-day average for water use is 22 gallons (83 l). When you include all uses for a person's benefit, such as irrigation, the worldwide average daily use is 475 gallons (1800 l). Meanwhile, Americans average about 100 gallons (378 l) and 1,350 gallons (5110 l) a day, respectively.

* It takes 2 to 7 gallons (8 to 30 l) of water to flush a toilet. The average American will flush the toilet around 140,000 times in his or her lifetime.

* It takes 2 gallons (8 l) of water to brush your teeth.

* You use 25 to 50 gallons (100 to 200 l) of water when you take a shower.

Experimental Summary

You'll install three different low-flow aerators on a faucet and measure the amount of water that flows each minute.

What You Need

- Kitchen sink
- Tape
- Dish tub (as large as you can get that will fit in your sink)
- Stopwatch
- Large measuring cup that has ounce (or ml) divisions on it
- Adult helper
- 3 faucet aerators from different manufacturers
- Tools, if needed for installation of faucet aerators

Experimental Procedure

1. Turn the water on at the level you usually use. Mark the point to which you turned the faucet with a piece of tape. This will ensure that you turn the water on at the same level for each trial.

2. Place the empty dish tub in the sink. Turn the water on to the level you marked in step 1. Let it run for 10 seconds. (Use the stopwatch to time it.) While you have the water on, hold your hands under the running water. Record your observations about how the force of the water feels.

3. Carefully pour the water from the dish tub into the measuring cup (you may have to fill the cup several times) to measure how much water was collected in 10 seconds. Record the amount of water in ounces (or ml).

4. Repeat steps 2 and 3 at least four more times, measuring the amount of water your faucet normally uses.

5. Have an adult help you install one of the low-flow aerators on your kitchen faucet. Be sure to read the directions.

6. Repeat steps 2 through 4 at least five times for the first aerator.

7. Remove the first aerator and install the next one. Then repeat steps 2 through 4, testing the water flow at least five times.

8. Repeat step 7 with the final aerator.

Conclusion

Average the amount of water that flowed through the faucet with no aerator. Average the amount of water that flowed from each of the low-flow aerators.

Water flow is measured in gallons per minute (GPM) (or in liters per minute), so you'll need to do a little math.

First, convert the average amounts of water to gallons. One gallon is 128 ounces. Divide the average amount of water by 128 to get gallons. (If you measure in milliliters, convert the milliliters to liters.)

Next, you need to predict how many gallons (liters) would flow from the faucet in 1 minute (60 seconds) instead of just 10 seconds. To do this, take the average amount of water in gallons (liters) and multiply it by 6.

So, if you measured 32 ounces of water in 10 seconds the GPM would be:

32 ounces /128 = 0.25 gallons x 6 = 1.5 gallons per minute.

Once you have calculated the GPM for your faucet normally and for each low-flow aerator, make a bar graph of brand versus GPM. Which low-flow aerator had the lowest GPM and which had the highest? How did the values you measured compare to those printed on the packaging?

Could you tell a difference in the flow of the water? What other observations did you make? Based on your experiment, which low-flow aerator do you recommend?

Take a Closer Look

How does a low-flow aerator make less water come out of your faucet? With air.

If you look carefully at most faucet aerators, you'll see a screen where the water comes out of the faucet. This allows air to mix in with the water and controls the flow. Some faucet aerators also shrink the opening of the faucet so that there is greater pressure. In either case, the result is less water coming out of the faucet each minute. Without an aerator, your faucet can run up to 8 gallons each minute, but a good aerator can reduce that to 1.5 GPM or even lower.

And where does all the water go?

World wide, most water (70%) is used for farming and raising livestock. Only 8% is used in homes for drinking and cleaning. The rest—22%—is used by industry for manufacturing. But if you look at just

the high-income countries such as the United States, almost 60% of fresh water is used for manufacturing. Next time you go to the mall, keep in mind that hundreds of gallons of water were used in making those designer jeans, mp3 players, and just about everything else you buy.

*Explore*Further

Monitor your family's water bill and see if there is a change in the amount of water used each month compared to before you installed the low-flow aerator and the other water saving plans found in the Take Action section. If there is a change, how much money are you saving? Does it cover the cost of the low-flow aerators?

Perform a similar experiment in the shower using low-flow showerheads. Which uses less water, a shower or a bath?

How much water does a drip waste? Let your faucet drip slowly into an 8-ounce (240 l) measuring cup. How long does it take the cup to fill up? How many gallons would the drip waste in 24 hours?

Dairy factories require a lot of water to make cheese and other products.

take action- - - ✈

After replacing all your faucets with low-flow aerators try these other easy steps to save water.

Keep it short.
If you can keep your shower to under five minutes, you'll save up to 1,000 gallons (3800 l) per month. You can also turn off the shower while you're lathering up.

Wait.
Don't run your washing machine or dishwasher until they're full to save another 1,000 gallons per month.

Reuse it.
Save the water you use to wash produce for watering the plants. If you use biodegradable soap, you can even put a bucket in the shower to collect water for the same purpose.

Do the dishes.
First off, wash or rinse the dishes in a basin instead of using running water—especially if you're then putting them in the dishwasher. In fact, with most newer dishwashers, you don't even have to rinse the dishes.

Check your pipes.
Insulate your hot-water pipes so you won't have to run the water too long to get hot water to the faucets.

Flush out water waste.
If your toilets are more than 20 years old, convince your parents to switch to low-flow versions. If you don't want to throw out the toilets, you can still reduce the amount of water used each time you flush. Fill a plastic half-gallon drink container (remove all paper labels) halfway with sand, gravel, or pebbles, and then add some water for more weight. Seal the container and place it in the tank away from all the moving parts. You could save 1 gallon (3.8 l) per flush!

Bottled Water

You're hot and thirsty—would you rather have a cold bottle of water from the fridge or throw an ice cube into a tall glass of tap water? Think twice before grabbing the bottled water. It isn't any better for you, and it's a whole lot worse for the environment.

People guzzle more than 41 billion gallons (154 billion l) of bottled water each year. They spend $100 billion worldwide and consume 2.7 million tons of plastic. The United States has the most sales of bottled water—26 billions gallons (98 billion liters). Italians drink the most bottled watered per person: on average, 51 gallons (192 l) annually. Some people drink bottled water because they think it tastes better; others think it's healthier, but most drink bottled water because it's easy to carry around.

The truth is that most bottled water isn't any healthier than tap water. And tap water in most industrialized countries is safe and can be run through a filter to improve taste and odors. In fact, about 40% of bottled water is actually tap water. It's just as easy to put filtered tap water in a bottle at home and carry that around. And it's a lot cheaper.

And the cost of bottled water is more than just money; it's also the impact on the environment. Most bottled water travels quite a distance, often half way around the world before it ends up in stores. This means trucks, planes, and boats burning gasoline, and releasing greenhouse gases. Then there is the packaging itself. Bottled water uses 2.7 million tons (2.5 billion kg) of plastic each year. A lot of that plastic, about 86%, ends up in landfills instead of in recycle bins.

So if you can, refill that water bottle from the tap. And start collecting other people's plastic water bottles to recycle.

Water Power

Before there were engines and electricity, people used water to generate power. Water wheels ground grain, cut timber, operated machinery, and more. They used the energy of water moving downhill—a clean, renewable, and green energy source. Could a technology that's more than 2,000 years old help us with our new energy needs? Or are we just spinning our wheels?

JUST THE FACTS

* Modern water wheels (called *turbines*) convert 90% of the energy from water into electricity.

* The most efficient power plant converts about 50% of the energy from fossil fuels into electricity.

* Hydropower generates about 20% of the world's electricity.

* Norway produces more than 99% of its electricity with hydropower.

* In ancient China, Emperor Ming of Wei used a water wheel to power his mechanical puppet theater.

THE EXPERIMENT
How does water speed affect the amount of work a water wheel can do?

Summary

You'll build an overshot water wheel and observe how much weight it can lift when the water flows over the wheel at different speeds. You'll change the water speed by pouring the water from different heights.

What You Need

- Scissors or utility knife
- 2 plastic milk jugs, 1 gallon (4 l) each
- 2 corks
- Wire coat hanger
- Wire cutter
- Hole punch
- Pliers
- String
- Thumbtack
- Film canister (or other small container)
- Tape (optional)
- Water
- Table
- Assistant
- Funnel
- Ruler
- Pennies
- Food scale

Build the Water Wheel

1. Use the scissors to cut the top off one of the milk jugs. Cut it just below the handle. Set the other milk jug aside—you'll use it later.

2. Cut five water-wheel blades from the top of the jug. Each blade should be a flat rectangle, 2 inches (5.1 cm) wide and as long as one of the corks.

3. Have an adult cut slits along the cork for each of the blades. Make sure the slits are evenly spaced. Slide the blades into the slits. Each should point straight out from the cork.

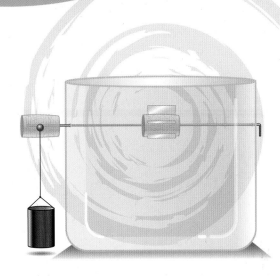

4. Straighten out the wire coat hanger. Using the wire cutters, cut off a piece that's at least 6 inches (15.2 cm) longer than the width of the bottom of the cut-up milk jug.

5. Poke the wire straight through the center of the water-wheel cork. This wire is the shaft.

6. Use the hole punch to punch two holes on either side of the milk jug bottom, about 1 inch from the top on opposite sides.

7. Slide the shaft through the holes so your water wheel hangs inside the bottom of the jug.

8. Slide the center of the second cork onto the shaft outside the jug. Use pliers to bend the other end of the shaft. A ½-inch (1.3 cm) bend will keep the shaft from sliding out of the jug.

9. Cut a 1-foot (30.5 cm) length of string. Use the thumbtack to attach one end of it to the top side of the cork outside the jug. Tie the other end of the string around the film canister. You can tape it onto the canister if needed. When the shaft turns, the string should wind around the cork and lift the canister.

10. See if your water wheel works. Fill the second milk jug with water and pour it over the water

wheel. When the water wheel turns, the string will wrap around the cork, lifting the canister.

Experimental Procedure

1. Place the water wheel on the edge of a table or counter so that the entire jug is supported. The end of the shaft with the cork and film canister should stick out so the canister can hang freely.

2. Fill the second milk jug with water. Have your lab assistant hold the funnel so that the bottom is 6 inches (15.2 cm) from the top of the water wheel. (Use the ruler to measure.) The funnel will ensure that the water falling on the water wheel is moving at constant speed. To make this work, you have to keep the funnel full of water.

3. Pour water into the funnel so that the water wheel turns and the film canister is lifted all the way up to the cork. Stop pouring water when the water wheel container is full.

4. Empty the water from the water-wheel container. Return the film canister to its original position and put a penny in it.

5. Repeat steps 2 through 5. Continue to add pennies, one at a time, until the water wheel won't turn.

6. Count the highest number of pennies the water wheel lifted. Weigh the pennies and film canister on the food scale. Write down the weight that was lifted.

7. Repeat steps 2 through 6 holding the funnel so that its bottom is 12 inches (30.5 cm), 18 inches (45.7 cm), and 24 inches (61 cm) above the water wheel.

Conclusion

Make a line graph of funnel height (x-axis) versus weight lifted (y-axis). The height of the funnel corresponds to the speed of the water. Every second water falls, gravity has more time to affect it, which means it falls faster. Its speed increases by about 10 meters per second (22 miles per hour). But as the water falls faster, it covers more distance, so it has less time to speed up. To double the speed of the water, you need to hold the funnel four times as high! How did the amount of weight lifted change as you changed the speed of the water? What other observations did you make during the experiment?

Take a Closer Look

Obviously, you can use falling water to lift pennies, but can you make electricity with it? Hydropower plants contain generators that turn the energy of the falling water into electricity.

Hydropower plants are built on rivers where there is a sharp drop in height, such as a waterfall. In most hydropower plants, a dam holds the water in a reservoir until it's needed. Hydropower plants don't

ExploreFurther

There are many factors that can affect how much weight your water wheel can lift. You could change the blade shape, size, and angle. You could adjust the number and placement of the blades. You could even use the scoop part of a plastic spoon instead of flat blades. How does changing the diameter of the wheel (the cork) affect the water wheel?

You can also change how the water hits the water wheel by adjusting the size of the opening at the bottom of the funnel. A smaller hole will let out less water than a bigger hole. What happens when you change where the water hits the wheel?

The wheel used in this experiment is called an overshot wheel because the water comes over the top of the wheel. You could also use this wheel as an undershot wheel by mounting the shaft in a length of house gutter (or a similar type of channel) and letting the water run under the wheel. This is how water wheels work in rivers.

store the electricity they make, so they only release water through the dam when they need to make electricity.

Inside the dam, the water flows through a pipeline, called a *penstock*, and onto the turbines. A turbine is just like your water wheel, except it's huge. Turbines can weigh more than 170 tons (154,000 kg) and turn 90 times per second. Most large dams have more than one turbine.

A shaft connects the turbines to giant magnets inside the generator. The turbine spins the magnet inside big coils of copper wire. As the magnets move, they create an electric current that flows through the coils of copper wire. Transformers and power lines deliver this electricity to your house.

What happens to the water? After it pushes the huge turbines around, the water is let out the other side of the dam through pipelines called *tailraces*.

But Is Hydropower Green?

While hydropower plants provide electricity without any pollution, there are still some major environmental side effects. Building a dam floods all the land above the dam, which impacts the plants and animals that live there. More algae and weeds grow in the river after it's been dammed, which makes it harder for fish and other underwater creatures to eat and breathe. In the northwest United States, salmon have to swim upriver to their breeding grounds. The dams block the rivers, so the salmon can't swim upstream to have their babies. In those areas, special channels are often built for salmon to swim through.

Often there are people living on the land that's going to be flooded to make the reservoir for the hydropower plant. The Three Gorges Dam in Yangtze, China—the largest hydropower plant in the world—created a reservoir that is 300 miles (500 km) across. More than 400 towns and villages were flooded, and more than 1 million people had to find new places to live.

Not So Fast Grass

Wouldn't it be nice if your lawn stayed short without mowing it and green without watering it? Drought-tolerant grass may be the answer. These grasses do well with less water and grow slower so they need less mowing. (Remember: This experiment isn't just about saving you a few precious hours of Saturday afternoon time. It will also help save the world.)

JUST THE FACTS

* In one hour of lawn watering, you use about 220 gallons (830 l) of water.

* In some places, homeowners water their lawns two-and-a-half times more than they need to.

* 50% of treated drinking water is used for watering plants outdoors.

* One-third of the world's population suffers from a shortage of water.

THE EXPERIMENT
How does the lack of water affect the growth of drought tolerant grasses?

Experiment Summary

You'll grow different types of drought-tolerant grasses and see how long they live after you stop watering them.

What You Need

- Permanent marker
- 12 small pots (small, used yogurt containers with three holes punched in the bottom work well)
- Potting soil with fertilizer
- Seed for three different drought-tolerant grasses such as: sheep fescue, buffalo grass, tall fescue, bahia grass, bermuda grass, seashore paspalum*
- Water
- Lamp with grow-light bulb
- Ruler

* You can find these seeds at garden supply stores.

Experimental Procedure

1. Use the permanent marker to label the pots with the type of grass you'll grow in each one. You'll have four pots for each type of grass, so label each with the name of the grass and a number (1 through 4).

2. Fill each pot with potting soil. Lightly pat the soil down so that it's about ½ inch (1.3 cm) below the top of the pot.

3. Carefully count out 40 grass seeds for each pot.

4. Sprinkle the seeds evenly in each pot. Check the label before adding seeds so you get the right seeds in the right pot.

5. Cover the seeds with a thin layer of potting soil—no more than ¼ inch (0.6 cm).

6. Water the pots. You want the soil to be moist but without puddles.

7. Place the pots under the grow lamp. Use the ruler to make sure the lamp is 12 inches (31 cm) from the top of the pots.

8. Water the grass lightly every day—use the same amount of water for each pot. The soil should be moist but not soaking wet.

9. In your lab notebook, write down when grass sprouts first appear in each pot. Continue to water the plants as normal until either two weeks after the last pot has sprouted or when the shortest grass is 2 inches (5 cm) tall (whichever comes first).

10. On this day, measure the height of the tallest grass in each pot. Stop watering all of the pots except for pot #1 of each type of grass. (This will be your control pot so that you can be sure the grass dies from lack of water and not something else.)

11. Observe your grasses every day. Write down any changes you notice, particularly when the grass not being watered turns brown and dies. Measure the height of the grass in each pot. Does it keeping growing after you stop watering it?

Conclusion

Count the number days between when you stopped watering each pot and the day all the grass in the pot was brown and dead. This is how long each type of un-watered grass survived. Calculate the average number of days each type of grass survived. Make a bar graph of grass type versus the average number of days. Which type of grass lived the longest? Which died first?

Average the heights of the un-watered grass for each type of grass on the day you stopped watering. Average the heights of the un-watered grass for each type of grass on the day you decided it was dead. For each type of grass, subtract the first height from the last height to find out how much the grass grew after you stopped watering. Make a bar graph of grass type versus height of growth after you stopped watering. Which grass grew the most? The least? How did the growth of the grass you stopped watering compare to your control pots?

Based on how long the grass lived and how tall it grew, along with your other observations, which grass do you recommend for use in lawns?

Take a Closer Look

Xeriscaping is a form of gardening and landscaping that reduces the use of water. The word comes from combining *xeros* (the Greek word for dry) with landscape. Xeriscaping was first used in desert areas where there isn't a lot of water available for watering lawns. Now that water pollution from fertilizer runoff and droughts caused by global warming have made saving water important to everyone, xeriscaping has become more popular.

*Explore*Further

Try this experiment in the real world. Get permission from yard owners with different types of grass. Stake out a 2-foot (0.6 m) square that will not be watered over the summer. How long will established grass survive without water?

Investigate other drought-tolerant plants besides grass, such as flowers, bushes, and other decorative plants. Compare the water needs of native plants (that grow naturally where you live) and non-native plants (that have been brought in from other places).

Explore how water gets to the plants. How does mulch affect the amount of water needed for plants? How does the effectiveness of drip irrigation compare to an old-fashioned sprinkler? How quickly does water evaporate from the soil?

take action

How else can you reduce the water used on your yard and lawn? Here are a couple of ideas.

Install a rain barrel.

Why not collect the water that lands on your roof and use it to water your yard? Set up a rain barrel to catch this water runoff and reuse it on your lawn.

Collect gray water.

Any water used in your house (except the water in your toilet) is considered gray water. This includes water from the sinks, showers, baths, and the laundry. Wash your dishes in a plastic tub and put a bucket in the shower with you to catch extra water (make sure you're using biodegradable soaps and shampoos). You can reuse this water for your lawn. The bacteria in the soil eats up the "gray"

part of the water so you don't need to worry about killing your plants. Use this water on ornamentals, your lawn, and only on the ground around vegetables. Don't spray it on the foliage of edibles.

Use soaker hoses.

These perforated hoses "leak" water along their length. Arrange sections of them around your plants and then cover with topsoil or mulch and leave in place. When you attach a regular hose and turn the spigot on low, water seeps out slowly right into the soil and mulch and soaks the ground where plant roots can access it quickly. When you sprinkle or spray water on plants, much is lost to evaporation.

Solar Still

Did you know that the Sun is a great source of water? Solar distillers or stills can provide clean drinking water using only the energy from sunshine. Stills are used every day by people all over the world who don't have easy access to clean water. During natural disasters such as hurricanes and tsunamis, solar stills are often the only source of safe drinking water for survivors. This project tests different designs of a solar still that creates drinking water from salt water.

JUST THE FACTS

* Under extreme conditions an adult can lose up to a $\frac{1}{2}$ gallon (2 l) of sweat in an hour.

* The average person can last without water for a few hours (under extreme conditions) to a week (under comfortable conditions).

* Arab alchemists used the earliest solar stills in 1551.

* The first solar still plant was built in 1872 for a mine in Chile and produced over 6,000 gallons (20,000 l) of water each day.

With this Solar Still Water Purifier from ClearDome Solar Thermal, dirty water is fed from the container on the side of the still into the trays inside. The Sun evaporates the water, which then condenses as clean water on the sides of the still (see close-up photo above). The clean water drips down the sides of the still and into the container on the ground. This still creates enough water for one person to live on for a day—as long as it's sunny!

THE EXPERIMENT

How does the material a solar still is made of affect how much water it can distill?

Experiment Summary

You'll make solar stills using different kinds of bowls to see which purifies the most salt water.

What You Need

- Ruler
- Water
- 3 bowls that are the same size and shape but made out of different materials (plastic or styrofoam, metal, and glass or ceramic)
- Salt
- Measuring spoon
- 3 plastic cups, 1 inch (2.5 cm) shorter than the height of the bowls*
- Clear plastic wrap
- Tape or 3 rubber bands large enough to go around bowls
- 3 small rocks
- Measuring cup
- Salt level test kit for ponds and aquariums (optional)**

* You can use a pair of scissors to cut the plastic cups to the right size.

** You can find these kits at pond and aquarium stores.

Experimental Procedure

1. Pour 2 inches (5.1 cm) of water into each bowl. Add 2 tablespoons (30 ml) of salt. Mix the salt water until all of the salt dissolves.

2. Place a plastic cup in the center of each bowl.

3. Stretch clear plastic wrap over the top of each bowl. Use tape or a rubber band to make an airtight seal.

4. Place a small rock on the center of the plastic wrap, right above the cup. Press down slightly on the plastic wrap so it stretches and sags down above the cup. Do this for each bowl.

5. Place the solar stills in the bright Sun. (The sunlight should be shining directly on them.)

They should be near each other but not touching.

6. After four hours in the Sun, remove the plastic wrap from the bowls and measure the amount of distilled water in each cup.

7. Write down your observations about the distilled water in the cups. How does it look and taste? If you like, you can measure the salt in the distilled water using a salt level test kit.

8. Wash and dry the bowls and the cups. Then repeat steps 1 to 7 at least three more times.

Conclusion

Average the amount of distilled water in the cups for each type of bowl. Make a bar graph of amount of water versus bowl type. Which type of bowl distilled the most water? Which distilled the least? How does the material the bowls are made of affect how much water was distilled?

What observations did you make about the distilled water? How did it look, smell, and taste? How does the distilled water compare to tap or bottled water?

Take a Closer Look

So how does that clean water get out of the bowl and into the cup?

Heat from the Sun warms up the salty water in the bowl. When the water gets hot enough, it evaporates, turning from a liquid (water) to a gas (water vapor). The gas rises into the air. The salt that was mixed with the liquid water doesn't evaporate. It stays in the bowl. When the warm water vapor hits the cooler plastic wrap, it condenses, turning back into liquid water. The water droplets stick to the plastic. Eventually gravity pulls the water droplets down, rolling them toward the rock where they collect and drip down into the cup.

Solar stills imitate the global cycle that water moves through. Sunshine heats water on the surface of oceans, lakes, and rivers so that it evaporates into the air. The water vapor rises up in the atmosphere until it condenses to water droplets in clouds. When enough water has collected in the clouds, gravity pulls the water back down to the Earth as rain.

The Watercone is a lightweight, mobile solar-powered water desalinator that can create up to 1.7 quarts (1.6 l) of safe drinking water a day. In the photo above, it's is being tested in Aden, a fishing village in Yemen.

*Explore*Further

What other features of your still affect how much water is distilled? What about the color of the bowl? Try using different colors of plastic wrap—you can get black from a garbage bag—to see what effect this has on the amount of distilled water.

Use other liquids besides salt water. Try muddy water, colored water, juice, soda, and even applesauce.

Try building a solar still from a simple hole in the ground. Dig a round hole that's deeper than your cup and about twice as big around as it's deep. Place the clean cup in the middle and a clear sheet of plastic over the hole. Secure the plastic sheet around the edge with rocks and place another rock in the center over your cup. The still will evaporate water from the soil and condense it into the cup.

A solar still created with a plastic sheet, a tube, and a shovel in Jackson Hole, Wyoming. Clean water collects in a container at the bottom of the hole and is sucked out.

Deadly Fertilizers

If you mention water pollution, most people think of big chemical plants pouring green slime straight into a river. But one of the biggest culprits in water pollution is fertilizer. That's right, the same stuff you put on your lawn and garden each fall and spring could be poisoning your water. Any rain that isn't absorbed by healthy soil ends up flowing downhill, eventually ending up in streams, rivers, or lakes. This water is called *runoff*. Any runoff that goes through your fertilized yard takes all the extra fertizlier with it. When this contaminated water reaches a body of water, it can create areas called *dead zones*—where fish and plant life die. This may not seem like such a big problem since we're talking about lawns and gardens, but think about how much fertilizer golf courses and cornfields use.

JUST THE FACTS

* There are at least 146 dead zones around the world.

* The largest dead zone is in the Baltic Sea and covers 43,000 square miles (70,000 square kilometers).

* The United States has the most identified dead zones in its coastal waters: 43.

* The dead zone in the Gulf of Mexico is about the size of New Jersey.

* A typical city block generates nine times more runoff than a woodland area of the same size.

* The United States has 330 million acres (130 million hectares) of farmland that produces food as well as runoff pollution.

THE EXPERIMENT
How does the type of soil affect the
amount of fertilizer in runoff water?

Adult
Supervision
Required

Summary

You'll fertilize different types of soil and collect the water that runs through the soil. Then you'll test the collected water for nitrates and phosphates.

What You Need

- Drill with 1-inch (2.5 cm) diameter bit
- 3 solid troughs or long window boxes (plastic or wood)
- 3 pieces of 1-inch (2.5 cm) diameter pipe, 2 inches (5.1 cm) long
- Silicone caulk or other watertight adhesive
- 3 or more of the following to fill the troughs halfway to the top: sand, soil, sod, gravel, clay
- Steps or a picnic table and cement blocks
- 3 clear, wide-mouthed 1-gallon (3.8 l) jars or buckets
- Water
- Fertilizer
- Watering can
- Measuring cup
- Water quality test kit with tests for nitrates and phosphates*

* Available at pool supply stores.

Experimental Procedure

1. Ask an adult to help you drill a 1-inch (2.5 cm) hole through one end of each trough. The center of the hole should be 1 1/2 inches (3.8 cm) from the bottom and centered between the sides.

2. Insert a section of pipe into each hole so that 1 inch (2.5 cm) or more extends from the outside of the trough. Seal each pipe in place with caulk or other watertight adhesive. Let the caulk set.

3. Fill each trough with a different material (soil, sand, sod, gravel, etc.) until it's 1 inch (2.5 cm) above the top of the pipe. The material should be about 4 inches (10.2 cm) deep. Each trough should have the same amount of material.

4. Use a set of steps or a picnic table and cement blocks to elevate the solid ends of the troughs 8 inches (20.3 cm) above the pipe ends of the troughs. The troughs should all slope downward at the same angle. Put a clear jar or bucket beneath each pipe.

5. Use the watering can to slowly water each trough with 1 gallon (3.8 l) of water. Water the entire trough evenly.

6. When water has stopped draining out of the pipes in the troughs, use the water quality test kit to measure the nitrate and phosphate levels in each water sample.

7. Measure how much water drained from each trough. Be careful not to mix (or mix-up) the water from the different troughs.

8. Clean out the troughs and repeat step 3. Following the instructions on the fertilizer package, fertilize each trough. Wait one day for the fertilizer to set.

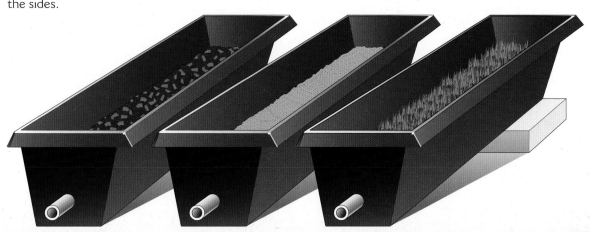

9. Repeat steps 4 through 7, testing the amount of nitrates and phosphates in the runoff of the fertilized material.

10. Repeat steps 8 and 9 at least two more times. Make sure that you clean out the containers and use fresh materials (soil, sand, sod, gravel, etc.) each time.

Conclusion

Average the nitrate and phosphate levels for each type of material you tested and for the control trial. Make two bar graphs to show your results, one for the nitrate levels and one for the phosphate levels. Put the average levels on the y axis and the type of material on the x axis. Don't forget to include the control trial.

How did the trials where you used fertilizer compare to the control trial? Which material gave the highest nitrate readings? Which material had the highest phosphate readings? Is this what you expected?

Take a Closer Look

Fertilizers help plants grow, much as a vitamin will help you grow and stay healthy. Fertilizers provide plants with three major nutrients: nitrogen (nitrates), phosphorus (phosphates), and potassium. Because most plants can suck up these nutrients best through their roots, fertilizer is usually applied to the soil.

The problem is that we usually put much more fertilizer in the soil than the plants can suck up. When it rains, the water washes the fertilizer into rivers and lakes or down into the ground water. In either case, we usually end up drinking this water, whether we get city water from lakes and rivers, or a well, which pumps up ground water. This type of pollution is also called *non-point source* pollution, because it comes from all over, not from one particular location. (Something like a factory that dumps pollution directly into a river is called a *single-point source*.) We don't really need to be drinking all the extra nitrates and phosphates, and they can cause health problems if we have too much of them. Really high concentrations of nitrates can cause *methemoglobinemia*, a deadly disease known as blue baby syndrome.

Too much nitrogen and phosphorus in rivers and lakes is dangerous for the plants and animals that live there. Basically, instead of making grass grow in your front yard, the runoff fertilizer makes algae and weeds grow in the water. This is called *eutrophication*. The algae and plants suck the oxygen out of the water as they grow, and when fertilizer speeds their growth, they suck up even more oxygen. Soon, there isn't enough oxygen left over for the fish and other organisms to breathe, so they die. All of these extra plants in the water can kill fish, keep you from boating and swimming in the water, and cause drinking water to taste and smell bad.

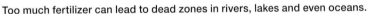
Too much fertilizer can lead to dead zones in rivers, lakes and even oceans.

take action

What can you and your family do to make sure that fertilizer isn't polluting your water?

Test the soil

Test your soil to find out exactly what nutrients your lawn needs. Apply fertilizer only when it's needed, during the right season, and in proper amounts. Or, even better, use native grasses that don't need as much fertilizer.

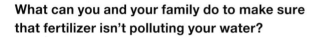

Apply carefully

Be sure keep fertilizers off the sidewalks and patios. Sweep any stray fertilizer onto the lawn or into the planting beds. Otherwise it will be washed directly into storm drains, which means directly into the rivers and streams.

Fertilizers aren't the only way pollutants get into our water. Here are a few others:

Dog poop

When you take your dog for a walk, be sure to scoop the poop. Poop is

chock full of disease-causing bacteria, nitrogen, and phosphorus. When you leave the poop on the ground, it'll get washed into the storm drains or nearby water tributaries along with all that bacteria, nitrogen, and phosphorus.

The car wash

The next time you wash your car, use these techniques to clean your car without dirtying the rivers and lakes. Use a bucket instead of a hose to save water. Use biodegradable soaps. Park your car over gravel or your lawn, so wastewater doesn't flow down the storm drain. Of course, the best place to wash your car is at a car-wash station where water is recycled instead of put into the ground.

Adopt-a-Street

Many communities have started programs called Adopt-a-Street. Volunteer for one of these programs (or help start one if your community doesn't have one). Collect litter, stencil warnings on storm drains, and talk to your neighbors about preventing runoff pollution.

More Interesting Stuff

Charts, Graphs & Tables

Charts and graphs are a great way to present your data. They look great on a display board and they organize your data in ways that can be understood easily and quickly. There are many different ways to create graphs and tables. Each type is good for showing off a different kind of data.

Data Tables

You've collected lots of numbers and you want to show them all off. But a data table isn't always the best way to do this. They're great for collecting data, but on your display board, a big table of numbers is really hard to look at! If you have four numbers or fewer, you can get away with a data table.

When you put your table together, be sure to label each row and column with units. Don't forget a title, too. The column on the left is for your independent variable, and the columns to the right are for your dependent variables.

Direction	Temperature Change (C)
North	3
East	5
South	10
West	6

Line Graph

You should use a line graph when your independent variable is a number or an amount. Line graphs are also used to show patterns or changes over time. The horizontal axis should always contain the independent variable, and the vertical axis shows the dependent variable or what you measured. Be sure to label the axes and don't forget the units of measurement! If you have more than one set of data on the same graph, use different colors or symbols for the different sets of data.

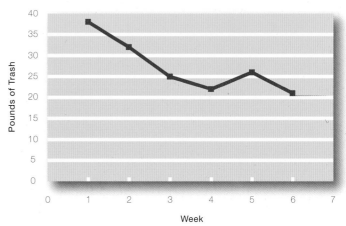

Trash from the Newcomb Family vs. Week

Bar Graph

When your independent variables are names or things rather than numbers, a bar graph is the way to go. The horizontal axis should always contain the independent variable and the vertical axis shows the dependent variable or what you measured. Be sure to label the axes and don't forget the units of measurement! Just like with a line graph, the horizontal axis should always contain the independent variable and the vertical axis shows the dependent variable or what you measured.

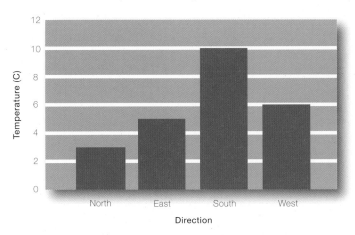

Pie Chart

Pie charts are used to show percentages or fractions. They are sometimes called circle graphs. The whole pie equals 100% and the different pieces of the pie make up the whole. Pie charts do not show changes over time. Label the percentages on your pie graph.

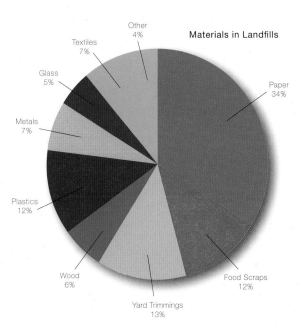

Sources

One of the most important things about being a good scientist is checking your facts. Scientists spend a lot of time repeating experiments (both their own and other scientists') to make sure that the data (or the facts) they've collected support their hypotheses.

As scientists figure out new ways to take measurements, and as we continue to live on the planet, the facts can change. So make sure to double- and triple-check them. Here's where the facts from our "Just the Facts" sections in this book came from.

Alternative Oils, page 14
First fact: http://www.climatecrisis.net
Second fact: http://www.msnbc.msn.com/id/18492185/
Third fact: http://www.worldwatch.org/node/808

Power Plants, page 19
Second fact: http://www.eia.doe.gov/kids/energyfacts/sources/renewable/biomass.html
Third fact: http://www.ehponline.org/members/2008/116-6/focus.html
Fourth fact: http://www.springerlink.com/content/u4g0044012063312/
Fifth fact: http://www.eia.doe.gov/kids/energyfacts/sources/renewable/biomass.html

A Bright Idea, page 22
First fact: http://www.ces.ncsu.edu/
Second and third facts:
http://www.homefamily.net/index.php?/categories/consumersmarts/light_bulb_energy_efficiency/
Fourth and fifth facts: *An Inconvenient Truth*
http://www.climatecrisis.net

Running on Air, page 26
First and third facts: Interagency Working Group on Hydrogen and Fuel Cells
http://www.hydrogen.gov/
Second Fact: http://www.hydrogen.gov/whyhydrogen_environment.html
The rest: US Department of Energy
http://www.eere.energy.gov/

The Sun Solution, page 30
Third fact: International Energy Association
http://www.iea.org/
Fourth fact: http://science.nasa.gov/
Fifth fact: Reported in *EV World*, June 19, 2004
http://www.evworld.com/article.cfm?storyid=709
Sixth and seventh facts: Solar Energy International
http://www.solarenergy.org/

Methane Madness, page 33
All facts: http://www.epa.gov/

Blowing in the Wind, page 37
First three facts: American Wind Energy Association
http://www.awea.org/
Fourth fact: Danish Wind Energy Association
http://www.windpower.org/en/core.htm
Fifth fact: Drachmann, A. G. "Heron's Windmill." Centaurus, Volume 7. 1961.

Putting the Sun to Work, page 41
First fact: Arizona Solar Center
http://www.azsolarcenter.com/
Third fact and fourth fact: http://www.uwsp.edu/

Out the Window, page 46
First and second facts: http://www.ces.ncsu.edu
Third fact: http://www.efficientwindows.org/energycosts.cfm
Fourth and fifth facts: http://www.eere.energy.gov

Garbage Diet, page 50
All facts: http://www.epa.gov/

Recycled Paper, page 54
First and second facts: "Handmade Paper"
http://www.theearthpaper.net/
Third fact: Lilienfeld, Robert and Rather, William. *Use Less Stuff: Environmental Solutions for Who We Really Are*. Ballantine Books, 1998.
Fourth fact: Food and Agriculture Organization of the United Nations   http://www.fao.org/

Is Bulk Better?, page 57
First fact: *Popular Mechanics*
http://www.popularmechanics.com
Second fact: Reported by *Telegraph Newspaper*
http://www.telegraph.co.uk/
Third fact: http://www.packaging-gateway.com/

Disappearing Waste, page 61
All facts: http://www.epa.gov/

Heating Up, page 65
First three facts: Pew Center on Global Climate Change   http://www.pewclimate.org/
Fourth facts: http://www.eia.doe.gov/oiaf/1605/ggccebro/chapter1.html
Fifth Fact: http://www.epa.gov

No-zone, page 70
First, second, and third facts: Nation Oceanic and Atmospheric Administration
http://www.ozonelayer.noaa.gov/
Fourth fact: http://www.epa.gov/air/

Lights Out!, page 73
First fact: http://www.flap.org/
Second fact: http://www.gsfc.nasa.gov
Third & sixth facts: http://www.newyorker.com/reporting/2007/08/20/070820fa_fact_owen?currentPage=1
Fourth fact: http://data.nextrionet.com/site/idsa/is125.pdf
Fifth fact: http://en.wikipedia.org/wiki/Light_pollution

Clean Up Your Act, page 78
First, second & fourth facts: Treehugger.com
http://www.treehugger.com/
Third and fifth facts: http://www.checnet.org/healthehouse

Down the Drain, page 84
First fact: *Encyclopedia Britannica*
http://www.britannica.com/
Second fact: U.S. Geological Survey
http://www.usgs.gov/
Third fact: http://www.epa.gov/
Fourth, and Fifth facts: http://www.allaboutwater.org/

Water Power, page 88
First four facts: National Hydropower Association. "Facts You Should Know About Hydropower." 1996
Fifth fact: Needham, Joseph. Science and Civilization in China: Volume 4, Part 2. Taipei: Caves Books, Ltd. 1986.

Not So Fast Grass, page 92
First fact: http://www.rwu.org/stats.htm
Second fact: http://extension.missouri.edu/
Third fact: Boulder Area Sustainability Information Network   http://bcn.boulder.co.us/basin/
Fourth fact: The Financial Times
http://www.ft.com/home/us

Solar Still, page 95
First and second facts: Scientific American
http://www.sciam.com/
Third and fourth facts: SolAqua
http://solaqua.stores.yahoo.net/

Deadly Fertilizers, page 99
First three facts: http://disc.gsfc.nasa.gov
Fourth, fifth & sixth facts: http://www.epa.gov

Greenwashing

Non-toxic, 100% natural, organic and Earth-friendly. If it sounds too good to be true, it just might be. Every day new products come out, claiming to be better for you and the environment. Do the products really live up to the claims their manufacturers are making? Sometimes they do, but often manufacturers are greenwashing—misleading consumers like you by listing environmentally friendly claims they can't back up. In fact, 99% of more than 1,000 randomly picked products showed evidence of some sort of greenwashing. (Source: www.terrachoice.com/files/6_sins.pdf)

Here are the six ways companies can greenwash their products:

1. The Hidden Trade-Off

More than half of all greenwashers suggest their product is green based on a single feature, ignoring bigger environmental issues. For example, paper towels, tissues, or copy paper may promote their use of recycled or post-consumer content but completely ignore the pollution that was released into the air and water when the product was made.

2. No Proof

If a manufacturer is going to claim their product is good for the environment, they should be able to back it up! Ask for the facts—responsible green products list a phone number or website you can contact to find out more. About 26% of "green" products don't even offer either of these things, so you can't check if their environmental claims are true.

3. It's Vague

Is the "green" product specific about what makes it environmentally friendly? Does the product just have a recycling symbol on it? What does that mean? Is it telling you to recycle the product or that the product is made from recycled materials? Can the whole product be recycled or just the packaging? This is just one example of a company being vague about their claims. Here are some more vague terms to watch out for:

- "Chemical-free"
- Nothing is free of chemicals—even water is a chemical.
- "Non-toxic"
- Everything is toxic if you consume enough—even water!
- "All natural"
- Poisons like arsenic, mercury, and uranium are all natural, too.
- "Green" and "environmentally friendly"
- What exactly do these mean anyway? Currently, there are no regulations to determine what can be labeled this way.

4. It's Irrelevant

Some environmental claims are just plain beside the point. So what if a product claims to be CFC-free? CFCs (chlorofluorocarbons) have been banned for 30 years. All products are CFC-free.

5. It's Lesser of Two Evils

The environmental claims are true, but they don't actually improve the health of people or our planet. For example, is it really healthier for a smoker to use organic cigarettes? Will applying "green" insecticides to your garden really reduce chemical runoff into streams and lakes?

6. It's a Little White Lie

Once in a while, manufacturers will just lie. For example, a dishwasher detergent may claim to be packaged in 100% recycled paper, but the container is plastic. Some shampoos claim to be "certified organic" but if you look at the label, you won't find any certification.

What can you do to make sure you don't fall for a greenwashing campaign?

Read the Label Carefully

Ask these questions: Does it tell you where to find more information about the environmental claims? Are claims made about just one small part of the product leaving the possibility of a hidden trade-off? Are the claims specific—and actually true? Could any similar product make the same claim?

Look for Eco-labels

The government and other organizations have set standards for environmental claims. If a product meets these standards, they should have an Eco-label on the packaging. EnergyStar, EcoLogo, and Green Seal are a couple of the most commonly used Eco-labels.

More is Better

Products that are truly environmentally responsible not only use recycled materials, they also reduce the amount of packaging or pollution in the manufacturing process. Look for products that try to improve the environment in many different ways.

Your Ecological Footprint

Have you every thought about how much impact you have on the Earth from your every day activities? Answer the questions below and add up your score to find out how many acres of land are needed to support the way you live—your ecological footprint. (Get your parents to help!) Adapted from: *Teaching Green – The Middle Years*

Question

Water Use	Answers/Points	My Score	Points I can save
1. My shower (or bath) on a typical day is:	No shower / no bath (0) Short shower 3-4 time a week (25) Short shower once a day (50) Long shower once a day (70) More than one shower per day (90)		
2. I flush the toilet	Every time I use it (40) Sometimes (20):		
3. When I brush my teeth	I let the water run. (40) I don't let the water run (0):		
4. We use water-saving toilets	Yes (-20) No (0))		
5. We use low-flow showerheads	Yes (-20) No (0)		
	Water Use Subtotal:		
Food Use			
1. On a typical day, I eat:	Meat more than once per day (600) Meat once per day (400) Meat a couple times a week (300) Vegetarian (200) Vegan (150)		
2. All of my food is grown locally or is organic	Yes (-20) No (0)		
3. I compost my fruit/vegetable scraps and peels.	Yes (-10) No (0)		
4. Most of my food is processed.	Yes (20) No (-20)		
5. Little of my food has packaging.	Yes (-20) No (0)		
6. On a typical day, I waste:	None of my food (0) One-fourth of my food (25) One-third of my food (50) Half of my food (100)		
	Food Subtotal:		
Transportation Use			
1. On a typical day, I travel by:	Foot or bike (0) Public transit / school bus (30) Private vehicle; carpool (100) Private vehicle; 1 person (200)		
2. Our vehicle's fuel efficiency is	More than 30 miles/gallon (-50) 24-30 miles/gallon (50) 17-23 miles/gallon (100) Less than 17 miles/gallon (200)		
3. The time I spend in vehicles on a typical day is:	No time (0) Less than half an hour (40) Half an hour to 1 hour (100) More than 1 hour (200)		
4. How big is the car in which I travel on a typical day?	No car (-20) Small (50) Medium (100) Large (SUV) (200)		

5. Number of cars in our driveway?	No car (-20) Less than 1 car per driver (0) One car per driver (50) More than 1 car per driver (100) More than 2 cars per driver (200)		
6. Number of flights I take per year?	0 (0) 1-2 (50) More than 2 (1000		
	Transportation Subtotal:		

Shelter Use

1. My house is:	Single house on large lot (50) Single house on small lot (city) (0) Townhouse/ attached house (0) Apartment (-50)		
2. Divide number of rooms in the home (no baths) by the number of people living at home.	1 room per person or less (-50) 1-2 rooms per person (0) 2-3 rooms per person (100) more than 3 rooms per person (200)		
3. We own a second, or vacation home that is often empty.	Yes (200) No (0)		
	Shelter Subtotal:		

Energy Use

1. In cold months, our house temperature is:	Under 15°C (59°F) (-20) 15 to 18°C (59 to 64°F) (50) 19 to 22°C (66 to 71°F) (100) 22°C (71°F) or more (150)		
2. We dry clothes outdoors or on an indoor rack.	Always (-50) Sometimes (20) Never (60)		
3. We use an energy-efficient refrigerator.	Yes (-50) No (50)		
4. We have a second refrigerator / freezer.	Yes (100) No (0)		
5. We use five or more compact fluorescent light bulbs.	Yes (-50) No (100)		
6. I turn off lights, computer, and television when they're not in use.	Yes (0) No (50)		
7. To cool off, I use:	Air conditioning: car (50) Air conditioning: home (100) Electric fan (-10) Nothing (-50)		
8. My clothes washer is a:	Top load (100) Front load (50) Laundromat (25)		
	Energy Use Subtotal		

Clothing Use

1. I change my outfit every day and put it in the laundry.	Yes (80) No (0)		
2. I am wearing clothes that have been mended or fixed.	Yes (-20) No (0)		
3. One-fourth (or more) of my clothes are handmade or secondhand.	Yes (-20) No (0)		
4. Most of my clothes are purchased new each year.	Yes (200) No (0)		
5. I give the local thrift store clothes that I no longer wear.	Yes (-50) No (100)		

6. I never wear _____ % of the clothes in my closet.	Less than 25% (25) 50% (50) 75% (75) More than 75% (100)		
7. I buy_____ new pairs of shoes every year.	0-1 (0) 2 to 3 (20) 4 to 6 (60) 7 or more (90)		
	Clothing Subtotal:		

Stuff I Use

1. All my garbage from today could fit into a:	Shoebox (20) Small garbage can (60) Kitchen garbage can (200) No garbage created today! (-50)		
2. I recycle all my paper, cans, glass and plastic.	Yes (-100) No (0)		
3. I reuse items rather than throw them out.	Yes (-20) No (0)		
4. I repair items rather than throw them out.	Yes (-20) No (0)		
5. I avoid disposable items as often as possible.	Yes (-50) No (60)		
6. I use rechargeable batteries whenever I can.	Yes (-30) No (0)		
7. In my home we have _____ number of Electronics? (Computer, TV, stereo, VCR, DVD, X box, Game boy, etc.)	0-5 (25) 5-10 (75) 10-15 (100) more than 15 (200)		
8. How much equipment is needed for typical activities? A lot=boat, snowmobiles, dirt bikes, etc. Very little=soccer, bicycling, etc.	None (0) Very little (20) Some (60) A lot (80)		
	Stuff Subtotal:		

Summary

Copy your subtotals from each section here and add them together for the grand total.

Water Use	_____
Food Use	_____
Transportation Use	_____
Shelter Use	_____
Energy Use	_____
Clothing Use	_____
Stuff I Use	_____
Grand Total	_____

What if everyone on the planet lived like you do? Is there enough land on the Earth to support your lifestyle for the whole world? To find out, divide your Grand Total by 350.
We would need _____ Earth's for the whole world to live like you do.

Multiply the number of Earths needed by 4.7 to get the number of acres used to support your lifestyle. Number of acres = _____ . This is how much of the Earth is used to provide the food, water, energy, and other resources you use—your ecological footprint.

What can you do to reduce the size of your footprint? You can get ideas from the questions above or check out the Take Action sections in this book.

Some average footprints:
United States: 24 acres
Canada: 22 acres
Italy: 9 acres
Pakistan: Less than 2 acres

Acknowledgments

I would like to thank the following folks for helping to make this book possible:

- Geoff & Sam Harris (my patient assistants) and Gina Barrer (safety guru)

- Orrin Lundgren, Shannon Yokeley, Avarind Teki, Dr. Larry Rome, Steve Shi, Deris Jeannette, Stephan Augustin, Dr. Max Donelan. Laurel Kohl, and Scot Case

- Special thanks to www.terrachoice.com for allowing us to reprint Greenwashing on page 106, and to the Institute for Sustainable Energy, Eastern Connecticut State University and the Sea to Sky Outdoor School for allowing us to reprint Your Ecological Footprint on page 108

Photo Credits

All photographs and illustrations, unless otherwise noted, are from Shutterstock.com.

Page 5, upper right: IStockphoto.com

Page 26: Hydrogen bicycle: © Shanghai Pearl Hydrogen Power Source Co., Ltd. Used with permission.

Page 45: Dr. Max Donelan and Biomechanical Energy Harvester: © Greg Ehlers/sfu. Used with permission.

Page 45: Dr. Rome with backpack: © Dr. Larry Rome. Used with permission.

Page 95: two bottom photographs: © ClearDome Solar Thermal. Used with permission.

Page 97: top: © Stephan Augustin. Used with permission.

Page 97: bottom: Photo courtesy of the U.S. Department of Agriculture, Agricultural Research Service.

Index